Shelter from the Storm

Shelter from the Storm

Caring for Victims from Kosova

Bruce Thompson

EPWORTH PRESS

Copyright © Bruce Thompson 2003

British Library Cataloguing in Publication data

A catalogue record for this book is available
from the British Library

Bible passages quoted from the *New International Version*
© 1973, 1978, 1984 by the International Bible Society.
Published by Hodder and Stoughton.

07162 0569 6

First published in 2003
by Epworth Press
4 John Wesley Road
Werrington
Peterborough PE4 7ZP

Typeset by Rowland Phototypesetting Ltd,
Bury St Edmunds, Suffolk
Printed and bound in Great Britain by
Biddles Ltd, *www.biddles.co.uk*

For Naim and Shpresa, Fadil and Valter who,
as interpreters, were our voices and ears,
and for all my other Kosovan friends
who enabled me to see and feel so much more
than I would have done without them

Contents

Kosovar Responses

Epilogue

Foreword

In September 2001 I had the privilege of meeting some of the people in this remarkable story. I shall not forget the Bogu-jevci, Hashani and Hoxha families, or their 'Mr Bruce', the author of this book, who with many others befriended the Kosovar Albanians who came as refugees to Manchester.

At one level, this is the story of a Methodist minister responding courageously to a situation which many of us would prefer to keep at arm's length. Such engagement is undertaken at personal cost and risk, and we are shown both in this book. At another level, it is a story which raises many of the great questions of our time: war and peace, relationships across boundaries (culture, language, politics, religion), and the involvement of the comfortable West with the rest of the world. And by his reflections upon experience Bruce Thompson provides essential raw material for the systematic thinking which such issues demand. The story, moreover, offers specific challenges to those engaged in Christian ministry: How are traumatized people to be comforted? How do Christians minister to Muslims – 'with Muslims' is perhaps part of the answer here – and what does evangelism mean in this context? How may other Christian communities learn from Timperley Methodists' experience of welcoming the stranger?

This is not a simplistic book – the questions are honestly faced, if not answered – and yet at its heart there is a simple conviction: 'Changing the world into the one that God has in mind is a tall order, but the world changes in me the moment I address my own fears and intolerance and care for my neighbour in need.' The author, I guess, would want to say that this is, above all, the story of the Kosovars, some of whom contribute moving testimonies. One of them memorably expresses the same conviction: 'I learned that if you love, you live' (Saranda Bogujevci).

There is love and life in abundance in this book. And so, for all the horror of the events which lie behind it, it is a story of hope. May it inspire others to see and to act.

Christina Le Moignan
President of the Methodist Conference 2001–2

Preface

To write about the events and experiences described in the following pages has proved a daunting task, but the responsibility I felt, both to the Kosovars who taught us so much and to the volunteers who encouraged me to produce a record, has kept me going, and I have tried to convey not only what happened but also what it felt like to be involved. At the same time, I have struggled to indicate how I was driven to examine my own motivation, to analyse the relation of this enterprise to my previous experience, and to reflect, in the light of what I was learning, about the character of my future ministry. Finally, I have been very conscious that, granted the present state of the world, others are likely to be faced by similar situations and that they can perhaps be helped by some of the lessons which we learned – about faith, about human nature, about organization and about the pressures which such an undertaking can generate.

For myself – and I am confident that I am not alone – I can testify to a vibrant conviction that God inspired our efforts, empowered our successes and understood our failures. As a result, I carry with me into the future both a new awareness of my own weaknesses, prejudices and limitations, and a new understanding of God's presence and activity in the world.

Bruce Thompson
23 April 2002
The third anniversary of the aid convoy from Manchester to Albania

Acknowledgements

My first thanks must go to those who encouraged me to write this account of the Meadow Court Reception Centre during and after the Kosovar war of 1999. Thanks to their example and advice, I realized that experiences which were deeply significant for all those involved could, if reported, be enriching for others too. David and Judy Adshead deserve special mention. Every moment that they could spare from running their own hair-styling business seemed to be spent at the Centre, David cutting hair and Judy chatting and listening. They really did work seven days each week! Moreover, Michael Farnsworth, Rabbi Brian Fox, Dr John Leonard and Canon Albert Radcliffe all said, having read my first draft, that the story should be made available to the widest possible audience. Their confidence in the venture and the deeply moving testimonies given at Shoah/Holocaust Conferences held in South Manchester helped to convince me that a record of what was involved in caring for victims from Kosova would be valuable for present use and future reference.

The book is dedicated to the interpreters, and I want to express my sincere appreciation not only to them but also to two other folk who spent some time at Meadow Court, Remzi and Saranda. Both are mentioned in the text. In their different ways, they were – and indeed remain – an enormous inspiration. Remzi has never allowed his confinement to bed to limit his friendship and support, and Saranda has displayed astonishing maturity in coming to terms with the terrible crime against her and her family. I never knew Saranda's mother but I am sure that she would be proud of her, as indeed Saranda's aunt would be proud of her cousins.

When Councillor Ray Bowker invited me to act as his chaplain, neither he nor I could have known how significant his mayoral year would be, but I am grateful that he persisted in his gracious invitation. The sustained contribution of the staff and volunteers at the local schools where the Kosovar children continued their education was invaluable and deeply appreciated; and thanks must also be extended to the Trafford Metropolitan Borough and all the other local authorities and governmental and non-governmental agencies throughout the country that welcomed Kosovar Albanians in the summer of 1999. I wish that they and all the British people could see for themselves the affection in which they are held by the Kosovars.

The Altrincham Muslim Association was quick to offer help at Meadow Court and I greatly appreciated their gracious co-operation. I offer my very best wishes, in particular to Iftikhar Awan and Amjad Latif, as they seek to build their community and strengthen the links with the neighbourhood.

I do not know what would have happened shortly before Christmas 1999, when everything seemed to be getting out of hand, if Bill Denning had not answered my phone call. I will never be able to thank him enough for being there when I needed him and for the understanding and encouragement which he offered.

Spending time with the Corrymeela Community in Northern Ireland during my 1995 sabbatical strengthened my resolve to challenge injustice and discrimination wherever it is found. It also steeled me for the efforts that would be required in standing alongside those who have felt the full force of prejudice and violence. A sign over the exit door at Corrymeela's Ballycastle centre read, 'Corrymeela begins when you leave'. I hope that, in a small way, I have managed to put that conviction into practice.

Lucy Kenyon typed the first draft of this book. It would have taken me years to type it myself, always supposing that I would have managed it at all! My thanks to her for getting the show on the road.

Without Graham Slater's commitment and his skills as an editor this book would not have become available. I owe him much from my student days when he was Principal of Hartley Victoria College, and my Kosovar friends and I owe him a great deal today.

Karen, David and Robert were wonderfully accepting of my preoccupation with the work of Meadow Court, especially in those first seven months. What can I say?

I want to place on record my appreciation of the help which I received from a number of books. Noel Malcolm's *Kosovo: A Short History* (Macmillan 1998) is a comprehensive history of the country and its peoples. In *The Fracture Zone: A Return to the Balkans* (Viking 1999) Simon Winchester records his travels throughout the Balkans as the war gets under way. Having read of his encounters with people and places, I often found myself, when visiting Kosova in 2001, experiencing a sense of déjà vu! An interesting look at the war itself is Michael Ignatieff's *Virtual War: Kosovo and Beyond* (Chatto & Windus 2000). For images of exile and first-hand accounts of experiences both in the camps and in the UK's reception centres I recommend *My Name Came Up: Kosovo, War, Exile and Return* (published by the Refugee Council in 2000). I mention in the text Neil Belton's excellent biography of Helen Bamber, *The Good Listener* (Weidenfeld & Nicolson 1998). Other biographies of those who faced extreme situations also helped me to come to terms with what I was hearing and feeling. These included *A Good Man in Evil Times: Aristides de Sousa Mendes* by Jose-Alain Fralon and the magnificent *Chasing Shadows* by Hugo Gryn, with

Naomi Gryn acting as editor (both published by Viking in 2000).

Lastly, and in a very real sense most importantly, I want to thank the Methodist Church and in particular the Methodist congregation in Timperley. It has become fashionable in some quarters to list what a person has done for the Church. I want it to be clearly understood that the Church has done far more for me than I could ever do for the Church. The people of Timperley Methodist Church rallied to the project without question or hesitation and went on to support the Kosovars so appropriately that there was never any concern that either too little or too much was being done (in my view, either fault would have been as bad as the other). Then, without any sign of complaint, they undertook more pastoral works themselves in order that I could be free to give whatever support was necessary to the residents of Meadow Court. Finally, I cannot imagine a more generous way of rounding off what I believe to be an important chapter in my life and in the lives of many more than the grant of a sabbatical to record this story and to visit Kosova.

May God's peace be upon you as you seek to challenge injustice and promote peace.

Introduction

It is important, at the outset, to say something about Timperley, something about myself and something about the historical background to the conflict in Kosovo.

Timperley is known to gardeners as a variety of rhubarb. It is also a village, originally rural but now suburban. During the nineteenth and early twentieth centuries, its market gardens helped to feed the expanding industrial city of Manchester, just a few miles to the north. Then, with the arrival of the railway in the 1930s, Timperley boomed and the leaders of its small Methodist congregation reacted to the situation boldly and wisely. Just a few yards from their existing building, built in 1847 and extended forty years later, they erected a much grander set of premises, in the heart of the now thriving commercial centre.

In recent years the buildings have been enlarged, and at present a thousand people use them every week, in groups both religious and secular. The Sunday congregation is large and diverse. While most of the worshippers come from a range of church backgrounds, Anglican, Catholic, Baptist, Methodist and many more, a fair number have little, if any, previous experience of church life. But all find a home there, and they seek to explore together what it means to be a follower of Christ in the modern world.

In its composition, the church membership, which has no particular theological axe to grind, truly reflects the character of the neighbourhood from which it is drawn. Though on occasion the church may be a focus of public attention – for example, by hosting a live TV broadcast of the Christmas nativity in 1995 – it prefers humbly witnessing for Christ and gently promoting the gospel in ways relevant to changing circumstances; and, to this end, its members are active in the many voluntary organizations within the local community.

This then is the community and this is the church which, at the end of the last war of the twentieth century, were able to draw alongside some of the most vulnerable people in Europe.

My own involvement derived from the fact that, for ten years from 1992, I was called to serve as the minister of Timperley Methodist Church. If, at the beginning of that period, I had been told what lay ahead, I would certainly have been unnerved and probably would not have believed it. But then, had I been told as a teenager that I would become an ordained minister, I would have been equally unnerved and would certainly not have believed it.

As I look back on my ministry, I recognize a pattern of change and growth. The changes are easy to state: I moved from a small mining town in the Midlands to multicultural Manchester to undertake my training, then from college to an inner-city circuit where I served three congregations, and finally from the inner city to a large, single congregation in Timperley. At every stage, it seems, a willingness to explore, even when such adventures have almost always terrified me, has helped me to grow and cope with things beyond my previous imagining.

A theological college may not be able to prepare its students for everything that they will face as serving ministers but it can provide basic tools and inculcate fundamentally important attitudes. In whatever circumstances I have been called to minister, whether supporting a bereaved family in East Manchester or standing with a bereaved father in the killing fields of Kosovo, I have tried to keep the tools which I received ready for use and to be open to all the opportunities for learning and serving which life has provided.

If the Kosovar refugees had found their way to this country during the early years of my ministry, I very much doubt whether I would have been able to give them the support which they needed. But, thanks to those who were patient with me as I took those first, tentative steps and those who taught me so much at each and every stage, I was better equipped to respond when the challenge came.

When I moved to Timperley in 1992, I knew nothing of Kosovo. Bosnia and Croatia, it is true, were beginning to become more familiar, and the break up of the former Yugo-slavia was prominent in the news headlines. But I doubt if many would have been able to point to Kosovo on a map. To this day, indeed, Kosovo remains a fairly isolated place, the size of Yorkshire. It is shaped like a diamond and land-locked by hostile neighbours and by Albania to the south-west. Before the conflict that erupted on to the world stage in 1999 Kosovo's population was reckoned to be around 2 million, 1.8 million ethnic Albanians, 200,000 ethnic Serbs and a very small number of Romanies and others. The vast majority of the Albanians were traditionally Muslim but, as a result of increasing secularization and the pressures of living in a Communist state for much of the last fifty years, non-practising. A small community of Albanian Catholics has played an important and effective role within society. The Serbs were principally Orthodox. Even the name of the country is contested. To Serbs, and interestingly to the Western powers now apparently anxious to make peace with what is left of the Yugoslav federation, it is 'Kosovo'. But to Albanians – and to us in the rest of this book – it remains 'Kosova'.

The history of the Balkans has been complicated and viol-ent. Indeed, it has frequently been punctuated by massacres and 'ethnic cleansing', even before the phrase was coined. The area has been the frontline and equally often, as successive empires have fought over its hostile mountains and fertile plains, the border between East and West. The clashes between Turks and Slavs, between the Ottoman and Austro-Hungarian Empires, sowed the seeds of the more recent violence. It was not lost on those political correspondents who covered the tragic events of the 1990s that the First World War began with an assassination in Sarajevo, Bosnia, the killer of Archduke Ferdinand, the heir to the Austro-Hungarian Empire, being aided by Serb extremists. Proud Serb nationalism and aspiring Albanian nationalism have been almost constant threats throughout the twentieth century and, while Bosnia and Croatia slugged it out, Kosovar Albanians were trying to win freedom from the oppressive Serb regime by non-violent means. It was only as frustration and discrimination increased to unbearable levels that the eruption that led to war occurred.

Little did I know as I celebrated the New Year in 1999 that, within a few months, Kosova would come very close to home.

Meadow Court

I

A Communion and a Convoy

*When loaves were thrown into the crowd from a cart
pulled by a tractor, everyone raised their hands to catch
them in a sense resembling man's prayer.*

John Hooper in Blace, Macedonia, *Guardian*, 3 April 1999

Looking back, I realize that my involvement was triggered
by a service of Holy Communion and a convoy.

The communion service was on Easter Day 1999 and at
that time, very soon after NATO's bombing campaign got
under way, Kosovar Albanian refugees were pouring across
the borders into neighbouring Macedonia and Albania.

In preparation for the service, I turned to a book of
devotions and found there a report of a small group of Christians sharing communion in a Latin American prison.[1] Their
homes had been broken up, their children were on the streets
and their parents and partners were in other jails. On Easter
Sunday they had neither bread and wine nor even water to
act as a substitute for wine. But that did not prevent them
from celebrating Holy Communion. Their mime of the reception of the elements was truly edifying for the participants
and deeply impressive for the non-Christian prisoners who
witnessed it.

In Manchester, the sixteen people gathering for early morning communion met in a more usual setting. But, having read
to them what had happened in the Latin American prison, I

invited them to consider, with me, what our hopes would be if we were refugees from Kosova. I was unsure, myself, whether bombing Serbia would be a help or a hindrance. But I knew that, if I was hiding in the forest while my wife and two small children trudged to an unknown destination and an uncertain future, I would want to know that, until the crisis was over, someone somewhere was prepared to offer them food, drink and accommodation.

Our Easter morning service continued and, at the point when normally the bread and wine would have been shared, I paused, suggesting that the elements should remain on the table and that, in order to express our solidarity with the Kosovar refugees, we should follow the example of the South American prisoners. Without exception, each person present broke off an imaginary piece of bread from an imaginary loaf for their neighbour, with the words 'The Body of Christ given for you', and passed an imaginary chalice, saying 'The blood of Christ shed for you'. All was done with unusual reverence and the service ended calmly but in a stunned silence. The sense of fellowship with friends we had never met was over-whelming.

Not long afterwards, a small group of people, who hap-pened to meet in a Flixton pub, decided that something should be done to help the Kosovar refugees. The church where the communion service had been held was invited to act as one of the many reception points for clothing and toiletries, and within a very short space of time a convoy of fifteen lorries was ready to leave Manchester for Albania. Similar responses to the crisis were being made throughout Europe and, while neither I nor any members of the church that I serve as minis-ter were directly involved in organizing the Flixton convoy, we were deeply affected by the local response to the appeal. Many people did very much more than empty their ward-robes of already discarded clothing. One child, for example, brought his favourite cuddly toy, a rabbit, for a Kosovar child who had no toys, and his action typified the spirit of costly generosity which prevailed.

The convoy left Manchester on 23 April, St George's Day, and I felt compelled to witness its departure. On the way to Flixton, I wished that I too could be on a lorry bound for the Balkans. As the crowds formed, the flags fluttered and the classes of school children lined up, there was inexpressible delight at what had been accomplished and, at the same time, desperate concern for those involved in the convoy's dangerous mission.

Standing beside one of the lorries, I placed a hand on its side and prayed. As I prayed for the drivers, the mechanics and those who would receive the aid, it dawned on me that a convoy like that has no room for passengers. Since therefore I do not have an HGV licence and am not a mechanic, a nurse or a doctor, what could I hope to contribute? Perhaps, as a Methodist minister, I could be more useful in England. Perhaps God had something for me and the community which I serve to undertake.

A communion service and a convoy, then, sparked a concern and a sense of expectation. But what God had in store for us still needed to be discerned.

When faced by other tragedies – for example, the shootings in Dunblane or the death of Princess Diana – we had held services of prayer and reflection, and that still seemed a good way to start. During the services on the following Sunday, therefore, I began to share with the congregations my belief that God had something for us to do. I announced that on the following Friday there would be a service of prayer and reflection, with a view to offering some kind of practical help to Kosovar refugees. Was it possible, I asked, that we could find a place in Timperley that could act as a temporary refuge? At the close of the evening service, Irene, who had been an evacuee during the Second World War, told me of Meadow Court on the Hale/Timperley border. It grieved her that, when people were in desperate need of accommodation, a fairly modern purpose-built facility should be lying empty. I raced back to the manse, jumped into the car and drove straight there.

Though I had lived in Timperley for almost seven years, I had never ventured down what appeared to be a road that went nowhere. Wellfield Lane was unique in our locality. It was so tranquil, especially at that time on a Sunday evening in late April, that I could have imagined that I had gone away on holiday. Spring bulbs were in flower and the buds on the trees were about to burst into bloom. The lane was narrow and winding, overshadowed by the hedges, and a small number of houses were dotted along its route. Then it opened out and there were allotments to the left and fields to the right. Meadow Court appeared like a mirage before me. Just an hour earlier I had not known that this place existed but, when I saw it, I could not believe my eyes. I did not doubt that I was looking at the very place we needed.

Meadow Court stood on the edge of a housing estate, overlooking green-belt land and opposite a well-equipped and almost new children's playground. Just a brief flight from Manchester airport, itself a five-minute car ride away, there were, I knew, many people sleeping under canvas. And here I was, standing in front of an ideal place of refuge. In my excitement and gratitude, I got out of the car and prayed that those who had been forced from their own homes in Kosova might come to feel at home here, however long or short their stay.

Back at the manse, I dashed to the study to ring the mayor elect, Ray Bowker. A year earlier, he had asked me to serve as his chaplain during his year as 'The Millennium Mayor' of Trafford Metropolitan Borough. At first, I was very hesitant about accepting. I did not feel, in fact, that formal occasions, especially formal civic occasions, were my scene. After all, not long before a TV producer, who had interviewed many members of the clergy in the course of his job, had told me categorically that I was not a 'meetings minister'! So I simply congratulated Ray on his election and expressed my hope that the exercise of his role during the millennium festivities would be especially satisfying. These wishes were warm and sincere. I really did want a special time for our world to be a special time for him. But what I didn't say was also significant. When four months later he repeated his request, I realized that he was either deadly serious or had tried others unsuccessfully! I agreed to serve as his chaplain, our relationship proved very important, and I remain grateful to him.

When I rang him on that April evening, Ray Bowker could not confirm what plans were or were not in place to receive refugees from Kosova, but he gave me the home telephone number of the man who, if refugees did arrive, would be responsible for their welfare. He, in his turn, could at that stage tell me little. But I did learn that, if Trafford were to be invited to take folk from Kosova, five or six possible reception centres would have to be considered and that one located in the north of the borough, i.e., closer to the mosques and the Town Hall, would be a likely choice. The geographical argument did not seem to me very strong, and I stressed the superior location of Meadow Court and the willingness of the church to use its minibus to transport refugees anywhere that they needed to go. I also emphasized the resources of the suburban belt, and the willingness of the churches to co-operate in offering whatever help was needed, free from proselytizing. At the end of the conversation, I was helpfully informed that members of the British Refugee Council were to visit the borough the following Friday, 30 April, to consider the options and that Meadow Court would be one of the centres they would look at.

Only hours after the visit to Trafford by the members of the British Refugee Council, our service of prayer and reflection for Kosova took place. We tried to make it as representative as possible, inviting two neighbouring ecumenical councils and partners in our own group of churches. Getting in touch with the relevant people was not easy; after all it was bank holiday weekend (as I was constantly reminded) and the notice given was very short (as I was also constantly reminded). I was informed, moreover, that one of the local churches was to have a 'Visitation', i.e., a visit from the archdeacon. I replied that he was welcome to join us!

Despite all the difficulties, no fewer than eighty people gathered at 8.00 p.m. on the Friday of the bank holiday weekend. Those present included our local MP and the mayor elect, both of whom had planned to be away with their families and both of whom were content simply to be there rather than take a leading role. Within the congregation the desire to do something was evident, and I used the opportunity to launch what I hastily termed 'The Kosovan Refugee Network', a grandiose and ambitious title for a group that, at that point, had no members. Because it was now likely that refugees would be housed in our neighbourhood, we needed, as a matter of urgency, to begin making preparation. And, to help those present to focus on what would be involved, I invited them to think of a much loved member of their own family, falling on hard times and needing assistance in setting up a new home. Granted the numbers of refugees who could be housed in Meadow Court, time, energy and expertise would be needed to gather not just clothing and household linen but also beds, washing machines, TVs, radios – in fact, everything found in a modern home. All the items, moreover, would have to be recorded on a database and brought into use as required. Leaflets, it was agreed, would be sent out to local clergy, to be distributed among their congregations, completed, returned and catalogued: a mammoth task but one which would, in the end, make the job of supplying material needs so much easier. But other needs would also have to be met, and the database would thus have to record language skills, details of relevant contacts, offers of friendship, and all the forms of expertise or practical help that could be of use.

It was planned that the service would conclude with the lighting of candles in the Garden of Remembrance in the church grounds. The location and the symbolism seemed very appropriate, but just as we were lighting the candles, a wind blew up and made it difficult to keep them alight. Fortunately, someone had the presence of mind to move the candles against the wall at the head of the garden. The patience of those who, subsequently, lit and relit the candles symbolized something which we only fully appreciated later. In launching the Kosovan Refugee Network, we had lit a tiny candle. Though vulnerable to the winds of misfortune, it would be tended by people of persistent faith who would ensure that, if extinguished, it was quickly lit again.

2

Preparations and Problems

Evening. We are in flight,
Plucking at the world of the clouds.
Beneath us a white kingdom
Azure triumph.
We speed on and pay no heed
To borders, armies, herds.

As if on the century's crest, we push aside
The mildew of history, the wars.
A lady shakes the sighs from her handkerchief
Somewhere over Mauthausen.

Evening. We are in flight.
Beneath us pensive
Europe drowses over serious matters.
Sleep on, wise lady,
Never bothered about your whims
Which were not mine.

Fatmire Kocmezi in *My Name Came Up*
(Refugee Council 2000)

The Refugee Council's representatives had been pleased with what they saw and it was soon decided that two centres should be opened, at Tamworth Court in the north of the borough and at Meadow Court. As I passed Meadow Court every other day, in my car or on my bike, I prayed that it would soon become a place of welcome, a safe haven, a home for those far from their homeland.

A preparatory meeting was held at the Town Hall on the morning of Friday 7 May. A sense of great excitement pervaded the overcrowded room, and it seemed that there would be no lack of voluntary helpers. It soon became clear, however, that most of those present were anxious to be involved in the work at Tamworth Court. It appeared, in fact, that, apart from myself, the only people eager to help at Meadow Court were two women from the Altrincham Muslim Association sitting next to me. Much of the initial discussion concerned Muslim dietary requirements and, granted my ignorance of Islamic law, I began to wonder how much I would be able to contribute. My anxiety was increased, moreover, when a Muslim expressed concern about the possible involvement of churches, fearing that they would use the situation for evangelism. To my relief the two women next to me rounded on him and, taking heart, I offered whatever help the Muslim associations felt would be appropriate.

The first flight was due to arrive some time on the evening of Tuesday 11 May and, on the previous day, I received a telephone call from the Town Hall requesting help in making up beds. When I walked into Meadow Court on the following morning, I realized that the half had not been told me. The beds, which were in flat packs, needed to be made before they could be made up, and there were many, many more things to be done.

The database, however, served us admirably. In next to no time, teams of people were on site: cleaning, hanging curtains, moving furniture. A sense of purpose overcame the threat of chaos and uncertainty, and great things were achieved. It was a pity that our awareness of what was expected of us unfolded through the repeated question, 'Why hasn't this been done?' But perhaps knowing everything from the outset would have taken just a little off the sense of fulfilment. Having to respond swiftly to ever-unfolding crises certainly made the whole enterprise more exciting.

Miraculously, the centre was made as ready as could reasonably be expected by the end of the day. But there was one last surprise. As I was preparing to leave at about 10 p.m., I became aware that we were expected to stay the night and be part of the welcome party.

It had been a long day. Having co-ordinated the volunteers, I had dashed to the Central Hall in the Manchester city centre to take a lunchtime service, and had eaten a sandwich while making phone calls to keep the work at Meadow Court on track. The last phone call had ended within a minute or two of the start of the service; and within a minute or two of its end I had headed for the tram back to Timperley. By 10 p.m., therefore, fatigue was setting in, and a real effort was required to focus on what a welcome party would need to do. Mike, one of our volunteers, and I checked with a WRVS member whether food would have to be provided, and she showed us a small tin of delicate sandwiches. They may even have been cucumber! After she left, Mike produced several loaves of cheese butties.

Conversations among the volunteers went on until the early hours. We shared our anxieties, reviewed the day, and realized that there was plenty to smile about. We reflected on the commitment that had already been made, recalling how, at a moment's notice, people had abandoned what they had planned to do. At the same time, we noted mistakes that had been made, and marvelled at what had been achieved.

The news that the flight had been delayed made us more keenly aware that the journey itself would be fraught with danger. How is air space obtained, we asked ourselves, when the skies seem full of war-planes? In such ways, the reality of war came home to us, and we were deeply fearful for those whom we were so anxious to help.

When my ministerial duties took me away from the centre

on the following morning, I realized that I felt more confident in the volunteers and less confident in myself. My personal anxieties had been increased by a phone call during the night. A Christian volunteer at the other centre, Tamworth Court, woke me with the words, 'Just thought you would like to know that the minibuses are leaving the airport.' I was beginning to realize how demanding, alongside my other work, involvement in the Kosovan Refugee Network was likely to be.

On the next day, therefore, I stayed away from Meadow Court. I told myself that the refugees needed space and would be overwhelmed if they had too many visitors at this stage. And that was doubtless true. But my own growing uncertainties probably played their part. In the end, I received a request for something – I can't remember what – and popped in, thirty hours after the refugees had arrived, to deliver it. I remember speaking to an interpreter, who had clearly rushed his shave because bits of paper were stuck all over his chin; and I recall a group of three men and a teenage boy chatting outside the main doors as I left. One of the men said 'Thank you', and the boy smiled as I put my thumb up. Such was my first brief encounter with four of the people who would help to change my life and my outlook on the world for ever.

Later that day, one of the women from the Altrincham Muslim Association rang to ask if we could discuss a co-ordinated response to the needs of the refugees. The request thrilled me. The last thing I wanted was to be seen as vying with others. So far as I was concerned, supporting the Muslim Association to get the job done effectively was much better than 'ploughing our own furrow' and getting praise for it.

The next day I met the two women in the church vestry. Their readiness to meet on our premises was a token of their genuine co-operation, and their attitude can be judged from the comment 'We are, after all, cousins in faith'. We agreed that the views of our new neighbours, not that we or others

might believe their needs to be, were paramount. And we
cemented our co-operation by a brief visit to the centre.

We did not stay long – only long enough to say hello to a
few folk and to receive requests for certain items. Thanks to
the database, everything asked for was supplied very quickly,
and thanks to the generous spirit which was abroad, the flow
of gifts continued unabated. I shall never forget the quantities
of nappies, stair-gates and children's clothing that confronted
me on the doorstep every time I returned home or answered
the doorbell. So much began to pour in that I wondered what
would have happened if there been no regulating mechanism
such as the database.

Indeed, as if to underline the issue, a contact from the
convoy team rang me, almost panicking, to ask if I could put
out an appeal for hairdryers. I gently asked how many exactly
were needed. Not knowing the number, she had put out a
general request to several churches. I have no idea how many
hairdryers were accumulated. But a more specific request
would have helped in two ways: effort to collect hairdryers
would not have been expended unnecessarily and the danger
of the recipients being overwhelmed by more than they
needed would have been reduced.

A phone call from a local churchgoer – one of a number
of calls which were singularly unhelpful – illustrated another
threat from which our efforts needed to be protected. 'Who
on earth do you think you are setting up this Kosovan Refugee
Network? Who gave you the right to do this? Under what
authority are you acting? I hear you have the Muslims
involved. There are other faith communities in the area, you
know. What about the Jews?' I pointed out that, as a member
of the Council of Christians and Jews, I would be more than
happy for the local synagogue to become involved. I also
indicated that I was chaplain to the Mayor, that everything
had been done with the approval of those responsible within
the local authority, and that no one else from the local

churches had apparently bothered. Finally, I thanked the woman for her call and told her that I would ring her back, should I need her assistance. The Kosovan Refugee Network and the database were designed to prevent such folk from bursting in, in their frustration and high dudgeon, with random forms of help.

There was one thing, however, which not even the database could do: prevent the centre from gaining the status of an unofficial tourist attraction. The road outside suddenly became a thoroughfare. Cars full of people, especially families, would drive slowly by with all occupants staring at the centre and anyone who happened to be there. One afternoon, I even saw someone drive up to take photographs. It was sickening voyeurism, but only to be expected in a society dominated by media coverage. Here, in the middle of our community, were representatives of the refugees featured day and night on our TV screens. How unsurprising, therefore, that a local church minister should pop into the centre and declare with excitement: 'This is wonderful; they all look just like those on the telly!'

3

Transformation Begins

Blessed is he whose help is the God of Jacob,
whose hope is in the Lord his God,
the Maker of Heaven and Earth,
the sea and everything in them –
the Lord, who remains faithful for ever.
He upholds the cause of the oppressed
and gives food to the hungry.
The Lord sets prisoners free,
the Lord gives sight to the blind,
the Lord lifts up those who are bowed down,
the Lord loves the righteous.
The Lord watches over the alien
and sustains the fatherless and the widow,
but he frustrates the ways of the wicked.

Psalm 146

The early days at Meadow Court, between the arrival of the first and second refugee flights, were filled with activity, and with uncertainty. People came and went, children ran up and down the corridors, and items were delivered. Vacuum cleaners worked non-stop, doubtless to relieve tensions and fears as well as to transform flats into homes; people packed into an office in order to make constant use of its telephone; and, on one occasion, a young woman, with her back to me, leaning sideways against a wall, indicated what could have been sorrow or fatigue or reverie, or a combination of all three.

And there were moments of potentially disastrous mis-understanding. When, for example, I was practising saying 'Hello' in Albanian, Petrit held out his hand, pointed to his chest and told me his name. Having responded by pointing to myself and saying 'Bruce', I promptly wrote 'Petrit' in my diary. To my astonishment, Anest, a young man sitting in the same room, immediately became very anxious and agitated. Fortunately, Naim, one of the interpreters, understood the situation in a flash and explained that there was nothing sinister in what I had done. I wasn't going to report Petrit to any authority. I was merely providing a note to aid my memory. Through this episode, I first became aware of the important role which the interpreters would play, a role which I appreciated more and more as time went on.

While we were awaiting the arrival of the second flight, valuable work continued to be done. Volunteers prepared rooms, set up a clothing store and completed a whole range of odd jobs. Moreover, having learnt a great deal from our initial experience, we were able effectively to pre-programme the work and to anticipate requests from the local authority.

We were able, too, to concentrate our efforts on areas that had previously been overlooked. We were asked, for example, to supply new underwear. How we failed to realize that it would be needed, I do not know. But we did and, because we had to respond quickly, I asked my church treasurer to request a £400 or £500 grant for this specific purpose from a fund containing £20,000. He reported back that a written request, outlining 'the parameters of expenditure', would be required. I was furious. But my bitter disappointment at this attempt to use official channels was soothed by the generosity of local individuals. As soon as word got around that we needed money, cheques and cash were pressed into my hands and pushed through my letterbox, often by people I had never heard of. The underwear – and later, as we shall see, some swimwear – was purchased.

Through this and several other incidents I gained new insight into human nature. When, for example, I informed a minister, at the outset, of my plan to distribute the database around the churches, he replied that it would be helpful to include his own name on it! Again, a church which failed to return the forms until six months later had, in the interim, retyped them, replacing the official titles and contacts with details of their own organization. And it was not only ministers and churches who disappointed. Despite the powerful appeals made by the media, others showed a disturbing lack of concern. One local store, on being asked for help in providing a few sheets and pillowcases, requested a formal letter. Anne, the volunteer who had approached them, raced round to track me down. I quickly put together a written request and, when Anne returned to the store, she was told it would have to be faxed to their head office! Anne patiently enquired if they could kindly do this for her. The response was, 'Sorry, we do not have a fax.' Anne finally trudged back to the manse and I faxed the request. The head office never replied.

But for every awkward minister, church and store, there were hosts of willing supporters. Anne had greater success with another store, where the manager ordered his staff to strip all the display beds and pack as much as possible into Anne's car. Ron, a retired accountant with a large toiletry company, filled the large boot of his car and his back seat with soap, toothpaste, shampoo, etc. from the staff shop. And local churches organized strawberry cream teas, coffee mornings and lunches – a very English response, but a very welcome one! Things were moving fast and going well.

At this time, a representative of the Altrincham Muslim Association and I arranged a meeting formally to introduce ourselves to the Meadow Court community and to ascertain any needs which so far we had failed to identify. Sylejman was the community's representative at this meeting. He had been beaten by Serb police as he sought safety for himself and his family. His teeth, or what was left of them, seemed loose as he spoke, and his leg had been damaged in the assault. He was bent double, hardly raising his head and rocking to and fro in an old chair.

We asked if the Kosovars would like us to arrange a trip. Sylejman raised his head, looked me straight in the eye and replied: 'We are not tourists. We are only here until the situation improves and we can go home.' It took me two years to learn the full meaning of this statement. It was a reaction, I discovered, to a remark by Zeljko Ražnatović, better known as 'Arkan', who was widely believed to be responsible for much of the ethnic cleansing in the Balkans. Claiming that the Albanians in Kosova had entered the country over the past fifty years, he had echoed the typical Serb attitude by describing them as 'tourists'. So far as Sylejman was concerned, however, Kosova was his home country. He had not been a temporary visitor there and he would not have paid a temporary visit to England unless forced to do so. Having made his point, however, he agreed that a visit to the swimming baths might be a good idea. The arrangements were duly made. Every Monday night for the next eighteen months a minibus arrived at Meadow Court to take those interested in swimming to the local leisure centre, and the provision of this simple but significant service proved very beneficial.

For many of the residents the need to purchase swimwear offered the first opportunity to leave the centre, and somehow the choosing of new items gave them new dignity. The effect was, in fact, quite remarkable, and one is humbled to recall it. Only men and boys joined me for the first trip to the swimming baths. There was a definite 'pack mentality' as we stepped out of the bus, and, on the short walk towards the baths, the Kosovars huddled together. I felt angry that people who presumably would have once walked a street alone without anxiety had been so affected by war.

As we entered the changing rooms together, the swimmers

from the church were already in the pool; and when we ourselves entered the water, we did so in a solid phalanx. Within
minutes, however, the boys separated from the adults and
relaxed in the presence of other youngsters. I had told everyone that the pool closed at 8 p.m. and at 7.50 p.m., as if a
signal had been given, the Meadow Court contingent vacated
the pool en masse, ten minutes before everyone else. And as
we walked back to the minibus, there was hardly a yard
between each person. I began to worry whether I was doing
the right thing. Was I asking too much of a clearly frightened
and perhaps traumatized group of people? I would only discover the answer to that question, I decided, by being with
them and sharing their fears and anxieties. As the minibus
emptied at Meadow Court, however, the expressions of gratitude confirmed that we were on the right course.

That night a seven-year-old boy with blonde hair and pierc-
ing blue eyes sat next to my own son David on the minibus.
In the following weeks, Fidan and David were to become
friends, and I shall never forget the first extended conversation
which, with the help of an interpreter, they were able to have.
Fidan was able to tell David of his escape from Kosova. Serb
troops had entered his school and, when the children fled, he
had hidden among trees, where his father later found him. It
was a vivid and moving story.

Over the next few Mondays, I learned to respond to
'Falemnderit' ('Thank you') with 'Ska per se' ('You're welcome'), and Petrit revealed a growing command of English
by gripping my hand and saying, 'Thank you for *everything*'.
At the same time, the 'pack mentality' gave way to a rush of
children and teenagers into the baths and a male-dominated
excursion was replaced by a mixed trip. The one drawback
was that the Albanian music in the cassette player was super-
seded by American rap!

It was always a delight to drive down Wellfield Lane and
see someone looking out for the bus from a first-floor window

or a small group rushing from the entrance with towels and costumes in hand. And it was even more pleasing to see someone who, when they first arrived, could not swim racing up and down the pool unaided.

Many of the residents at Meadow Court, however, remained concerned about people close to them who had been unable to escape. Naim, for example, was anxious about his sister. He turned to me, pleadingly, with the words, 'My sister is in Kosova. Do you know who can help me to get her out?' During my interview with Sylejman, Naim had made clear to me, with a sudden surge of emotion, just how terrible was the persecution in Kosova under Serb rule – university lecturers being removed from their posts, schools being closed, innumerable individuals being intimidated and murdered. I now discovered that his sister and brother-in-law and their two children were heading for the border. Their hope was that they would be able to cross over into Bosnia and obtain permission there to join Naim in England. I was moved by the trust in me which his appeal for help revealed, and by his evident distress. I can picture him now in the swimming pool, his back against the side, his arms resting on the floor and his eyes wide and unfocused. I was desperately anxious to help. Unfortunately, however, after much effort and many, many phone calls, letters and appeals, the happy outcome we all longed for could not be achieved. As a result of the war, Naim's sister suffered from stress and experienced a breakdown, and Naim was deeply affected by her plight. Nothing could be done. I felt frustrated and even overwhelmed by the trauma that surrounded me. But the more I came to know about the people at Meadow Court, the more determined I became, despite growing tiredness, to do more to help them.

By contrast, what happened to Elvis brought much joy to us all. Elvis had been engaged to Arlinda before the war, but she had been visiting friends in Serbia when NATO's bombs began to fall. Having gone into hiding until the war ended, she was able to cross over into Hungary and finally to obtain a visa to come to the UK. When Elvis and Arlinda, a Catholic, married in February 2000, they chose to have the ceremony at the Methodist church. This was to be our first Albanian wedding.

Elvis's name, when first heard, was capable of producing a smile on many faces but his outsize frame and matching personality were welcome on any occasion. I recall one incident that first produced a near panic, then stunned me into silence, and finally caused me to chuckle at the audacity involved. While I was sitting with his family, Elvis and Astrid, his cousin's husband, came to ask where they could get a replacement for the leaking petrol tank in Astrid's car. I gave them directions and they left the room. Half an hour later, I went into the car park, to find them standing next to Astrid's silent car. Thinking they needed a lift, I offered to take them to the garage. My invitation was declined, however. They would go, they said, in Astrid's car. 'But,' I replied, 'I thought the petrol tank was leaking.' 'It was,' I was told, as Astrid started the engine, and I developed anxieties about the leaking fuel. 'It's OK', said Astrid, opening the bonnet and tapping the washer bottle. 'I thought it was the petrol tank that you wanted to replace.' 'Yes', said Astrid, again pointing to the washer bottle. 'The petrol is in here.' He and Elvis, having filled the washer bottle with petrol, had run a tube from it straight to the carburettor!

Elvis and Arlinda's great day was a wonderful occasion. Most of the residents of Meadow Court were there, and many people from the church came to support the happy couple. Jean, one of the church members, arranged, through her daughter, for Arlinda's wedding dress to be just right and everything went without a hitch, with Naim again acting as interpreter. Jean also arranged for a caravan to be available on the Welsh coast for the honeymoon; and Patrick, an old friend from college and the minister in that part of Wales, made sure that a taxi collected Elvis and Arlinda from the railway station and took them to the site. On hearing that they were Kosovar refugees on honeymoon, the taxi driver, Elvis later informed me, ran them to and from town, whenever they wanted, for practically nothing.

I received almost as many photographs of this wedding as of my own, and they will always bring back happy memories. But other aspects of the occasion produced mixed emotions. For example, I will never forget the rehearsal. Naim respectfully refused to translate the vows into Albanian, judging that they were far too important for a non-minister like himself to articulate. He helped us out of a difficult situation, however, by suggesting that he write them down in Albanian for Elvis and Arlinda to read aloud. 'Fine,' I said, 'but on Saturday you will have to wear a cassock like me!' Naim, not realizing that I was joking, willingly agreed. So long as he did not have to say the important words, he was happy. At the ceremony itself, I felt the poignancy of the occasion. Before me were a couple who had been wonderfully reunited in the aftermath of war, while beside me stood a man in an agony of distress about his sister and her family. I wondered what Naim was thinking and feeling at that moment.

Naim was an excellent interpreter, as were his wife, Shpresa, and Fadil, their colleague in the early days. Each was able to communicate feelings as well as words. When I grew accustomed to punctuating sentences with a pause for interpretation, the limitations of translation began to be overcome, and soon both I and the folk at Meadow Court felt confident enough to move to another method. We would give to Naim, Shpresa or Fadil a whole story or picture and trust them to get the meaning across. Every last word no longer needed to be translated. But the pressure placed, in this way, upon the interpreters was very considerable.[2] Naim, Shpresa and Fadil were absorbing and expressing the emotional burdens of everyone present, and that was too much to ask.

They willingly worked long hours, without thought of their own welfare. We owe them much, and I very much doubt if we will ever be able adequately to express our gratitude.

4

The Banquet of Life

Hunger, in its stark and visible forms, touches a chord in us because our own bodies, our own experience, enable us to relate in some way to the hungry. Our experience of God's goodness in our own lives, and in so much that we know of [God's] goodness to others, equally convinces us that we are not doomed to sit by helplessly while we watch our hungry sisters and brothers die. Hunger, like the poverty which causes it, is not inevitable. We can make a difference. We can know a joy God intends for us – that of being both host and guest at the banquet of life.

Mary Evelyn Jegen SND, *How You Can Be a Peacemaker*
(Liguori, Publications 1985)

It was a balmy summer evening, just three weeks after the first Kosovars arrived at Meadow Court. I was about to go on holiday and Naim and Shpresa, the two interpreters, were kindly meeting with me to review the programme of support already in place and to consider how requests for help could best be handled while I was away. We were sitting on white plastic garden chairs around a matching table .(all donated, of course), eating fresh melons and drinking chi (Albanian tea). As we relaxed in what could have been our own open-air cafe, the continuing war seemed a long way away.

'Why do you do this for my people?' asked Shpresa. I wasn't surprised at the question. A great deal had been accomplished, and it was understandable that, at some point, curiosity about the effort involved should find expression. But I paused before replying. I had not needed to question my own commitment to the cause or to consider my motivation. Granted my Christian faith, I could hardly have responded in any other way. But if I replied at this point in specifically Christian terms, would Shpresa understand? We had only known each other for a little over a fortnight, and the project still had a long way to go. Better opportunities more adequately to explain my involvement would, I felt, be certain to arise. So I simply said, 'Because we are all God's people', and waited for Shpresa's supplementary question, but it never came. Her initial enquiry, however, touched me deeply, not least because it arose out of genuine curiosity and was unaccompanied by any hidden agenda.

On reflection, those earliest days at Meadow Court may have been more wonderful than I then realized. Obstacles were overcome, friendships were forged, and in remarkable ways 'coincidences' kept on occurring. My faith is such that I have never looked for immediate answers to prayer. I believe that God's responses are sometimes delayed, often unexpected and usually only discernible with hindsight. However, I found myself beginning to expect the surprising and to anticipate the unexpected!

Material needs seemed to be supplied in next to no time. For example, Adrian had begun keyboard lessons and needed an electric piano. At synod, a few days later, I learned of a church which had a spare one requiring a new home! This was twelve months after the arrival of the first flight and 'coincidences' had been happening throughout the intervening period. My dreams were being realized before my eyes, and it was very exciting. It was also strange, outside my previous experience – yet very natural. How did it relate, I asked myself, to my early life and to my passionate concern for all victims of cruelty and injustice and, in particular, those who suffered in the Holocaust. Such questions, as we shall see, preoccupied me more and more as time went by.

Meanwhile, there was much to be done. Initially, the material needs of the Kosovars had been paramount. They had grabbed what they could carry before the militias torched their homes. The primary task, therefore, had been to provide clothing and accommodation. But there is a limit to the amount of clothing which can be stored and used, and once those who had spent weeks under canvas had a roof over their heads, other needs had to be met.

It became clear that the Kosovars wanted to engage in their own community activities. One of their first requests was for a table-tennis table. But where on earth could we get one? The church table was of poor quality and a new one would be expensive. At the same time, Shirley, a lay worker in a local church, phoned to tell me that she had arranged for the teenage boys to attend a football coaching course run by Manchester United. Boots would be needed, and she wondered if we had any money. I did a quick calculation in my head and realized that something in the region of £150 would be needed. As I put the phone down, it rang again. The caller was Jim, a member of a neighbouring church whose help had already been invaluable. 'Bruce, we had a collection at church and I have £150. The folk would like it to go to something specific. Is there anything we need?' Then, as I absorbed this amazing news, he added, as an afterthought: 'Oh, someone says that they have a table-tennis table. I don't suppose it's of much use, is it?'

Having purchased the boots, we realized that kits were also needed and that new ones were desirable. We could have easily rung around and obtained second-hand kits, but for teenagers only the latest kit will do; and we certainly wouldn't have wanted to make it easy for anyone to play 'spot the refugee'. But how on earth could we afford new kits for eight teenagers? Then it struck me that, through Anne, a member of one of my previous churches in East Manchester, we had contacts with the club. Would Manchester United provide the kits? Within a day or two, the person responsible for their merchandising operation had cleared our request. I was to take the boys into the megastore and kit them out, compliments of the club! The 'raid' was to take place on Bank Holiday Monday, and the merchandising director gave me his personal mobile number in case we ran into difficulties. We didn't. The trip was amazing. The boys looked on in shock as the shop assistant loaded them up with the latest shirts, shorts, socks and even shin pads. The realization that each shirt was priced at the equivalent of a month's salary for a teacher in Kosova added to the shock.

Manchester can be a great place for teenagers, whether they like football or not. But for eight Kosovar teenagers, fresh from the horrors of war and the squalor of refugee camps, it seemed almost too good to be true. I was later to discover that, although most of the passengers knew that they were coming to the UK by the time they boarded the plane at Skopje, they only learned fifteen minutes before touchdown that they would land in Manchester. When this was announced, a loud cheer went up among the boys!

I can understand their joy, even though I am not a Manchester United fan (some friends describe me as an ABU – Anyone But United). Manchester United will never know how much joy they brought to those boys when we visited the megastore. My letter trying to express their appreciation certainly did not do it justice. One thing is certain: even the most ardent fan's joy at winning titles could not surpass the exhilaration of these most recent kit-wearing fans from Kosova.

The night on which United won the European Cup came a close second in the excitement stakes. The second flight of

Kosovar refugees had just arrived, and as the two teams played out the drama of the match, I was sitting, with some of the boys and many of the men, around the TV set in the community lounge at Meadow Court. No matter how exciting the match was, and clearly some of those present on that night gained much from briefly escaping the thoughts of home and missing loved ones, at least two of us could not escape the drama going on all around us. Nesim, a man of great dignity and integrity, pondered the scene and perhaps the events of recent days: 'If only the whole world could reflect the community we have here at Meadow Court.' If only. But our new-found community was certainly a microcosm of Kosova: city dwellers and villagers, professionals and artisans, driven from their homes but still together.

No wonder Shpresa was prepared to ask, 'Why do you do this for my people?' In the coming months, I asked similar questions about others. Why did those who were so willing at the outset become so reluctant later? Why did those who were willing to support worthy causes abroad, by cheques or short-term personal service, overlook the project on our doorstep? Why did those who wanted to help restrict our new friends by managing them?

Where the last question is concerned, it was enlightened to read, eight months after Meadow Court opened, *The Good Listener*, Mark Belton's biography of Helen Bamber, founder of the Medical Foundation for the Care of Victims of Torture. In her teenage years, Helen worked alongside survivors of Belsen shortly after liberation. Many were kept and 'managed' at a former Panzer barracks just a short distance from the concentration camp. It seems that, even when we act with the best intentions, our instinct to control is so strong that we manage people rather than empower them, supervise rather than liberate them, oversee rather than support them.

At the same time, I tried to explore my own motives. Was

I fascinated by the novelty of the task? Or looking for kicks? Or thinking that participation would look good on a future CV? Or hoping to get a book out of the experience? I struggled with these issues, but the biggest struggle of all was to keep the process of welcome and rehabilitation, of hospitality and renewal on track. But for now I was to let go. No matter how much I would miss Meadow Court, a holiday in Ireland beckoned.

Karen, the boys and I adore Ireland, a country with a rich and often tragic history, but full of life and with hopes of a better future. We stayed in County Clare, in a cottage on the shores of Lough Derg, and the countryside looked as beautiful as ever. My mind, however, was so full of Meadow Court that it was difficult for me to relax. I could now put names to faces that had filled our television screens, and I could picture vividly what was involved in escaping to neighbouring refugee camps through forests and mountain passes. As I went for walks in the evening, my mind was filled with images of frightened people fleeing the terror of ethnic cleansing, of women on tractors and men on mules. I recalled, too, the effect of such scenes on our younger son, Robert, just six years old. We had watched an old man fall from a donkey which his son was leading into the mud of a forest; and we had heard a teenager, with his young brother on his shoulders, explain that a clown's performance was all right for children but could not take his mind off the war or his missing parents. Shortly afterwards, as Karen and I had gone into the kitchen, we turned around to see Robert standing in the doorway weeping.

As I walked along the track adjacent to the cottage, I tried to put myself into the shoes of a man carrying all that he could for as long and as far as he could. The weight, the anguish, the fear, the loss – all were real to me. Even more poignant was a visit to a mass grave of those who had died in the Great Famine. How many more mass graves, I asked myself, would there be in Kosova? When we took a trip to Holy Island on Lough Derg, the boatman, referring to the famine, asked 'Where was the Church when we needed it?' Where, I asked myself, was the Church in Kosova? Where had it had been as nationalism in the Balkans continued to rise? Where had it been when racism took the form of ethnic cleansing? If not there, I consoled myself, then at least at Meadow Court and countless other places where the hungry needed food, the homeless shelter, the naked clothing.

The war seemed to end abruptly. We returned from a day trip and the boys switched on the television to watch a children's programme. David came scurrying into the kitchen. 'Daddy, the bombing has stopped!' It seemed like a dream. Tony Blair's promise to the Kosovar Albanians in the camps that they would go back to their homes could be fulfilled. There was still much to be achieved, as the tense stand-off at Prishtina airport between Russian paratroopers and their British counterparts proved. (General Jackson was later to report that we could have started World War Three there and then.) And, being so far from Meadow Court, I found it difficult to cope with what was still a very confused situation. I could only imagine what was going on in Timperley as the news broke.

I recalled Isobel Hunter, a wonderful woman whom I had met in Northern Ireland in the summer of 1995, just a few months after the ceasefire. Isobel worked for the Cornerstone Community on the Springfield Road in Catholic West Belfast. She had spent years working for peace, through bereavement support and children's work, only to find herself on holiday in Germany when the IRA ceasefire was announced! It was with a resigned smile that she told me how she watched Gerry Adams and the rest march past her home on the Springfield Road on German television news. All that she had worked for seemed to be coming to fruition and she was not there to witness it in person. Her loss, needless to say, was greater than mine, but now I could better understand her feelings, and my smile that night in Ireland must have rivalled hers four years earlier.

The party that was arranged at Meadow Court a few weeks later was an occasion to savour. An Albanian flag fluttered on one side of the entrance, a Union flag on the other. Elvis had rigged up a tape deck and speakers to play music from his first-floor bedroom window. Ylber was looking every bit the barman in white shirt, black tie and trousers. And Remzi, as he always did, sat quietly observing.

Remzi never ceased to amaze me. Paralysed from the waist down since a car accident in 1985, he sat in his wheelchair near the gates to Meadow Court, staring into the fields opposite as residents and staff, volunteers and visitors, came and went. As the months progressed and summer gave way to autumn and autumn to winter, Remzi spent less time outside and more time in his bed. But there he grappled with English and, without formal tuition, became so fluent that a time came when I knew where I could go to talk. He had a wealth of wisdom, accumulated from years of reflection, and I greatly valued his advice. All of us, after all, need people who hear beyond the words that we utter, who understand the feelings that are not mentioned as well as those that are expressed. Such folk have always made time or been forced to set time aside for reflection. If, in addition, they have wrestled with thoughts of what might have been, they will be either very bitter or very mature. Remzi was a man who, though prevented by circumstances beyond his control from realizing his full potential, retained a zest for knowledge and a thirst for history – and was, for me and for many others, an invaluable friend and confidant.

There are many folk who feel that, as they grow older, they have less and less to give. But they have had, and they continue to have, time for reflection, time which, by our busyness, we deny ourselves. As their lives draw nearer to an end, therefore, their time, time for passing on the fruits of a lifetime's experience, is precious, and we should value the time we can spend with them. This is not to say that today's emphasis on the creative imagination of youth is misplaced. But it is to say that, if progress involves retaining everything of value, we need also to tap into the wisdom of age.

Remzi seemed subdued at the party, and others too – for example, an elderly woman in full Albanian costume and a young woman with a child at her side – smiled only occasionally. But all around them the party atmosphere was deeply rich and wonderfully free. Life, for that brief moment, looked exhilarating. I stood back and observed, and David, our older son, then aged eight, never left my side. 'This is an important night,' I told him as we drove to Meadow Court. 'Try to remember it.'

As I held him by his shoulder, I contrasted our good fortune with what Banush, Remzi's brother, had told me earlier. He and I had stood in the small shelter, kindly erected by the Scouts, and Banush had explained, through an interpreter, that in the camp at Stankovic he and his family, like many others, had lived, eaten and slept in a tent smaller than this. How good it was that the present structure was decorated with bunting and Christmas lights and that rows of tables were covered in food from front to back, side to side. 'This is like a wedding,' said Naim, and I wondered then if he was contemplating popping the question to his girlfriend Shpresa. They married later in the year.

Jesus likened heaven to a banquet prepared for all people. In that image, there seems to be no place for distinctions of creed or culture. Perhaps this party, then, was a glimpse of heaven. Great things had certainly been accomplished: the lowly had been lifted up, and the hungry fed. I had once heard a Jesuit priest, who had worked in the shanty towns of South America, say, 'The poor know how to party.' Now from personal experience I know that he was absolutely right.

Perhaps for this reason, among others, we who are rich are called by God to do what we can, so that the poor may party, and we can all celebrate without guilt or shame.

5

The First Farewells

For every sunrise, a sunset;
For every hello, a farewell;
For every birth, a death.
In all of these, God is with us.

Only a few weeks after the bombing campaign ended, the media focus shifted. In 1999, after all, the civil war in Indonesia came hot on the heels of what happened in Kosova, and the cameras and the crews that operate and support them were relocated. As a result, predictable, and often pointed, questions began to be asked. 'So, what are you (i.e., the Church) going to do about Indonesia?' 'Why are we still concentrating on Kosovans when others are now in trouble?' 'Why am I still feeling guilty that others are hurting while I'm living the life of Riley?' 'Why are the Kosovans still here?'

The continuing presence of the Kosovars became a frequent talking point towards the end of the summer. Doubtless, at that stage, people did not pause to recall why they were here in the first place. It was easy to remember how they had fled oppression, hidden in basements, boarded crowded trains, trekked through mountain passes and squatted – under canvas, if they were lucky – on the Macedonian border. But how did they come to be on our doorstep? The answer was simple: the great British public had willed it to be so.

The images of children crying, old men dying and women queuing at border crossings had captivated the television audience in what we know as 'the West'. A war fought in a highly technological age is bound, thanks to communications and propaganda, to have its armchair voyeurs. Through newspapers, magazines, television and radio our minds and imaginations were bombarded by images of ethnic cleansing and its consequences. Indeed, one journalist suggested that the memories of the Holocaust which were triggered fuelled our moral sensibilities. How right he was! If, during the previous decade, we had ignored ethnic cleansing elsewhere in the Balkans, now was the time to say that enough was enough. Hawkish politicians could typically conclude that, once again, appeasement had failed and that force was the only realistic response. Whether the bombing increased the ethnic cleansing of Kosova or only increased the flow of Kosovar Albanians into neighbouring countries is difficult to determine. What is clear is that far fewer people were killed in Kosova than died, while the West deliberated, in Bosnia. Even so, whatever our judgement about the justice of NATO's campaign, we were faced, as we prepared to celebrate the dawn of a new millennium, by an enormous humanitarian crisis in the heart of Europe.

So it was that the governments of the 'free world' began, somewhat reluctantly, to 'invite' refugees into their countries. This, after all, was what the all-important opinion polls were suggesting that the voters wanted and, in a democracy today, it is not leadership that matters but the will, and the whim, of the people. The trouble is that, where democracies are shallow in their values and lack the capacity truly to care for their neighbours irrespective of their colour, creed or culture, mood swings are apt to occur. At such times, what is called for is a leadership that acts, as the prophets did, with a real vision of what God intends. Prophets may not be able, any more than others, to see into the future. What sets them apart is their ability to see how God's continuing will and purpose may best be served.

Most of us have poor memories when it comes to international crises. Unless events impinge directly upon us, yesterday's 'displaced persons worthy of refugee status' become, for us, today's 'bogus asylum-seekers scrounging everything that the state will provide'. It was inevitable, therefore, that the public mood, positive and welcoming at first, should become indifferent and even hostile later. I recall that, when the first families began to return to Kosova, Angie, one of our church members, seized the opportunity to obtain for every family high quality suitcases at a fantastically low price. Not many suitcases were needed at that point but she knew that such generous offers would not be available for long. In the same way, the enthusiasm of those who set out with good intentions to help at Meadow Court faded with the passage of time. I remember asking Sylejman if he had seen a particular person, someone who had been very involved at the beginning: 'No, Mr Bruce, you were among the first to welcome us, and you'll be the only one left to wave us goodbye.' An exaggeration, I am sure, but kindly meant and very perceptive. Staying power and consistency seem in short supply in modern life.

Those, moreover, who do 'stick it out' have to be prepared to face hostility. David and Judy, for example, gave invaluable help to the Kosovar families and David, a hairdresser generous with his expertise, was immensely popular at Meadow Court. Late one night there was a loud knock at their door and literature from the British National Party was pushed through the letterbox. The material, which expressed vehement opposition to the presence of Kosovar Albanians, was not received, it seems, by anyone else in David and Judy's street.

I gave up counting the number of times I was asked 'Are they still here?' or worse still, 'So when are they going home? I thought the war was over.' Serb aggression in Kosova was over, yes. But fear, anxiety, grief, healing of broken bodies and disturbed minds – all these continued. Every single family resident at Meadow Court had good reason to be there. They were not just fleeing oppression, seeking a roof over their heads and food on hastily provided tables, worthy enough though such reasons are. Within each family there was at least one person in urgent need of the kind of medical attention that can only be provided by a state such as ours.

Take, for example, the Hoxha family. Two of their three children urgently required medical care, and both had been in hospital in Kosova. Adrian was an acute asthmatic who suffered greatly in the Kosovar environment and, given the post-war pollution, would find living there a life-threatening prospect. Adriana was just 24 when the war broke out and had been married six months. She had apparently been healthy until the exodus from her home in Ferizaj, but by the time she reached England she was very sick. Even so, the first time that her husband, Amir, heard the word 'leukaemia' was when paramedics climbed aboard the plane when it touched down. They had come to take her directly to hospital.

There were very few opportunities for Adriana to acquaint herself with her new surroundings. She had often wanted to come to England and was frustrated that, now that she was here, she could not explore the places of her dreams. But, though she had to spend most of her days in Manchester Royal Infirmary, she was able to share an important expedition to the historic city of Chester.

Once the war had ended, Sylejman, who had earlier informed me that the Kosovars were not tourists, took up the suggestion of an outing for the Meadow Court community. In next to no time, Jim, who had already provided furniture, taken on many odd jobs and generally done far more than could possibly have been expected of him, had booked a coach, and almost all the residents set off on a memorable expedition. Sometimes the phrase 'excitement in the air' is overused but it perfectly describes the atmosphere on that bright and sunny July morning. The coach did not offer the most luxurious transportation you have ever seen, but it had been provided at a wonderfully low rate because of the exceptionally high quality of the passengers. The Methodist church in Chester also did us proud, splitting us into three groups for a guided tour which ended at the cathedral. What could have been a brief walk through that ancient place of worship became a rich and rewarding experience lasting an hour. All were awed by the vastness of the roof and the intricacy of its carvings, and Anest, an Albanian Catholic, was moved to tears as he sat quietly in a pew.

Once we had arrived in the cloisters, the joy of the occasion was clearly evident, and the group photographs – the biggest photographs of the community ever taken – were treasured throughout the families.

As we walked to the Methodist church for lunch, conversation flourished. It was still limited by our dependence on help from our interpreters, but in that cosmopolitan city centre, among languages from all around the world, there was no longer any need to hide the fact that Albanian was a rare language on the streets of England. It was just another language to be heard and accepted as different from our own.

There was, however, one anxious moment. We suddenly realized that Mrs Hashani, Remzi and Banush's mother, an elderly and frail woman in full Albanian costume, was nowhere to be seen. It seemed that, in the joy of the moment, her absence had been overlooked. Banush and I raced back along the streets to the cathedral, but we could find no trace of her. By the time we returned to the Methodist church, panic was beginning to set in. I was wondering how on earth even the most caring and discerning police officer would be able to discover who Mrs Hashani was. To my profound relief, I found her tucking into a cheese sandwich!

It had been a truly memorable and moving day. Rexha, reluctant to climb back into the coach, offered me a role reversal. 'Mr Bruce' – I had grown accustomed to this respectful title, favoured by adults who disapproved of teenagers calling me 'Bruce' – 'I will be a Methodist minister, you go back to Kosova!' It was a telling moment, a snapshot of contentment and acceptance. Rexha had expressed his desire to stay, yet he was later to become one of the first to return to his homeland.

Saying goodbye as the first folk to leave Meadow Court prepared to fly home to Kosova was far from easy. There were many tears and kind words and, on each occasion, I was implored to visit Kosova one day. But sadly there was one person I would never be able to visit in her homeland.

The visit to Chester was Adriana's first major excursion after her arrival in England. The hospital had permitted her a temporary discharge, and while the trip meant a great deal to everyone else, it was extra special for Adriana, her husband and her family. How she managed to smile so serenely when she must have been exhausted is beyond me. From time to time I am privileged, in my work, to meet people like her, and on every occasion I am rescued, all too briefly, from pettiness and complaint. Every community needs its Adriana.

A few days earlier, she had been so radiant at the party at Meadow Court that at first I had failed to recognize her. As I later realized, she had worn a wig, and had been introduced by Amir as his new wife. I honestly thought that he was pulling my leg, and that she must be a friend or a visitor. As the evening gave way to night and fatigue overtook the dancers, her delight illuminated the ever-increasing darkness of the marquee.

Now, as she was wheeled round the busy streets of Chester, baseball cap on head, she glimpsed what she had been missing and, at the same time, gave us insight into the courage of the condemned. Within three months, Adriana was dead: her strength sapped, her sparkle dimmed, as life drained from her.

In her brief time among us, Adriana graced our world,

touched our lives and left us a legacy. We will cherish our memories: of her poise at the party, her love for her family and for life itself, and her reproachful 'tut' when her father sounded the minibus horn to hurry swimmers to the baths. Particularly poignant for me were the phone calls I made from holiday to try and encourage her to go on, and the joyful greetings and tearful farewells in the isolation room where she spent her last weeks.

Her father Sadri and I stood at the window on the top floor of the hospital, overlooking the city. The clash of architectural styles – Victorian splendour and post-modernist maze – was as confusing as the situation in which we found ourselves. Sadri had had little time to add English to his wealth of languages; what little time he had had was spent with his now dying daughter. We stood, therefore, without exchanging words, and in truth speech was unnecessary. Looks, sighs and silence said it all. As I drove him back to Meadow Court, with Adrian on the back seat, we passed the university. Sadri pointed and said, 'Adrian', expressing his hope that Adrian would one day study there. The past was about to slip behind us and the future to be faced.

Adriana's illness may well have been brought on by the stress of war. She was, therefore, a victim in a double sense – by being forced to leave her country and, though her wounds were not immediately evident, by suffering physically. We recognize, when we see burnt out buildings or broken bodies, how terrible the impact of war can be. But we must never forget the grief of those whose loved ones are maimed or killed. Their trial continues.

It took weeks to arrange for Adriana's body to be transported back to Kosova, and for Muslims such a delay is especially distressing. One of the most important and most difficult matters was ensuring that the Hoxha family would be permitted to return to the UK. They had come here not only because of Adriana's condition, but also because of

Adrian's acute asthma. It was vital for him to stay here and thus to avoid the life-threatening atmosphere of post-war Kosova.

The negotiations, in which the church and I were willing to get involved, proved long and complex. Thankfully, with the help of the local authority, all fell into place and, knowing that they would be allowed back into the country, Amir and the Hoxha family flew out with Adriana's body. She was returning to her homeland, but not in the way that she had hoped. It was Thursday 11 November 1999, an important day for those who remember the victims of war and the sacrifices that have been made to overcome evil and see justice done. The date was significant not only for Adriana's family but also, as we shall see, for the rest of the Kosovar family at Meadow Court.

6

Remembrance

Whoever plants a tree and looks after it with care until it matures and becomes productive will be rewarded in the hereafter.

If anyone plants a tree or sows a field and men, animals or birds eat from it, he should consider it as a charity on his part.

From the *Sayings of the Prophet Muhammad*

It was 11.00 a.m. and light rain was falling. We had not all gathered but, as I had come to appreciate over the preceding months, precise punctuality is not, for many people, a high priority. And yet all those involved recognized that it was an important occasion. For recent events had given Remembrance Day a significance in the Kosovar calendar which it had never possessed before.

The residents of Meadow Court were desperate for every scrap of news from Kosova, and the newly acquired satellite TV set in the communal lounge provided pictures and information which were not judged suitable for British prime-time consumption. The images of destruction on the streets of Gjakova and the other towns, villages and hamlets of the Drenica valley left little to the imagination.

Why then was Syljeman seen so often frowning in concentration, with his short-wave radio pressed tightly to his ear? What information was he needing that the TV coverage did not supply? The answer is – lists. Lists of the missing, wounded and killed – and lists of the found. Day after day, from a radio station in Tirana, the latest lists would be read out.[3] Sylejman's brother and two nephews were missing. Small wonder that, if he was not walking around seeking the best reception, he was seated at a table in a suitable spot, with his head inches from that radio. Small wonder, too, that better quality short-wave radios were highly prized and, when provided by kindly supporters, greatly appreciated.

The way in which our work at Meadow Court was bound up with events in Kosova was further underlined by an article in the supplement of a Sunday newspaper. It recounted how, in the Macedonian town of Tetova, a photographer named Izmai Luta had been taking passport-style photographs and providing an ad hoc identity card for those refugees who had been stripped of documents. It was an unequivocal but gentle reminder that people were of value, that their identities mattered and that they could not be robbed of their dignity. At that point (6 June), he had photographed no fewer than 26,879 Kosovar Albanians. Just a tiny number were featured in the article, which I took with me to Meadow Court. After a glass of orange juice and chi, I produced the cutting from my bag. The effect was staggering. Because Tetova is near the Kosovar border, some of the residents recognized a number of those whose photographs had been reproduced. There was great excitement as Amir and his father Nesim pointed to people whom they knew and for whom they could even provide family case histories!

One day, Sylejman was not outside with his radio. When I arrived at Meadow Court, half a dozen people were sitting at a table and on a nearby wall, and there was a sombre atmosphere. Yllka quietly informed me that Sylejman had received bad news. His brother and one nephew had been found, shot and rammed down a well, with the remains of a dog and a cow on top of them.

On entering Sylejman's flat, I was ushered into his bedroom. It was, as ever, immaculate, with everything neatly in place, almost as though expecting a military inspection. Sylejman sat on his bed with Ylber next to him. Both rose to welcome me. Sylejman held me tight, having kissed me on both cheeks. Had I been told six months before that, so soon afterwards I would be naturally exchanging such a greeting, I would have cringed and expressed incredulity. There had been no room in my upbringing for such physical affection. But here I was, embracing a man who wept for those he loved and now knew that he would not see again – at least, not in this life.

Over the years, I have learnt that, in dealing with the bereaved, speech is of limited value. 'At such a time, a thousand words are not enough, but one may be too many.' I cannot remember where I first read this sentence and I may not reproduce it absolutely accurately. But it has influenced me greatly, and its wisdom is confirmed over and over again. A Methodist deaconess, for example, took up a new appointment and learned immediately of a family who had suffered a bereavement. She visited them, found the experience emotionally draining and felt that she did not find the right words to say. For years afterwards, she feared that she had failed that family. Then she met someone who greeted her warmly, saying, 'You won't remember me but you came to visit my family when my dad died. You were wonderful.'

Further confirmation is provided by a young man in Northern Ireland. When he had just taken up a post as an assistant minister, he received a request to visit a woman whose son had just been killed. Unfortunately, his senior colleague was not available and, with some apprehension, the young assistant called on the woman. She was understandably heartbroken and began to question the young man about why a loving God should permit her son's death. The young man drew on his knowledge of Christian approaches to suffering but soon ran out of steam. Just as the woman began to bombard him with yet more questions, there was a knock at the door. The young assistant, breathing a sigh of relief at the sight of his colleague, felt that he was about to learn what to say in such difficult circumstances. But the minister walked in and, without a word, threw his arms around the grieving mother.[4]

Effective care for those who mourn does not depend on words, or theological qualifications, or even a common language. Neither Sylejman nor Ylber could speak English, and about my Albanian the less said the better. But at that moment there was no barrier between us.

The manager of Meadow Court graciously asked me if I would conduct a memorial service for Sylejman's family. On reflection, I wondered how I could do so without the occasion being so overtly Christian as to offend those refugees who still clung to aspects of their Islamic faith. I was also concerned not undermine our co-operation with the Altrincham Muslim Association. In the end, I came up with the idea of planting a tree.

Sylejman greeted the suggestion with obvious joy, and within a few weeks meetings were held to discuss where and when the tree should be planted. Thanks to the local authority, a nearby park was chosen, a tree provided and a plaque produced. The ceremony was to take place on Thursday 11 November at 11.00 a.m. and many guests were invited: local civil dignitaries, staff at Meadow Court, volunteers and neighbours. The occasion was not only to mourn those killed in the war, but to remember those who were missing and to give thanks to the people of Trafford for their welcome and hospitality. It took a while to agree on the wording on the plaque, and we finally settled on the following: 'This plaque commemorates the care and protection of the United Kingdom towards 62 Kosovar Albanians who took refuge at Meadow Court during and after the 1999 war, and in memory of all those who were killed or were forced from their homes by the Serb Chetnik forces.'[5]

By the time we had all assembled in Halecroft Park, the rain had ceased. It was as if nature itself was indicating that, after the fall of many tears, it was now time to reflect quietly. The busyness of Meadow Court earlier that morning was now replaced by stillness. There was a crowd much greater in number than I had envisaged, seemingly in blocks: before me, the civic officers and staff; to their left, volunteers; then neighbours and family; and finally, on my right, my friends from Meadow Court. It was a sombre and serious occasion, and every word had been carefully crafted. Not everyone could hear or understand what was said, but the occasion spoke for itself and would be remembered as truly eloquent.

After a brief welcome and introduction, the Beatitudes were read, followed by an expression of thanks by Sylejman. Then a teenager from Kosova and a child from England, the latter being the daughter of a member of the Altrincham Muslim Association, ceremonially planted the tree, an English oak. I had actually wanted the Association to play a fuller part in the occasion, but Sylejman insisted that, as the form of the ceremony had been my idea, I should conduct it entirely. This made me feel somewhat uncomfortable, but I was thrilled to see that the Association was well represented. Before we began, Iftikhar, the Secretary, had kindly given me a card with two sayings from the Prophet Muhammad on the planting and care of a tree. They were so appropriate – they are to be found at the heading of this chapter – that I included them in the ceremony.

After saying a few words, the Mayor removed the Albanian flag to reveal the plaque. There followed a reading from the Qur'an ('O you who truly believe, seek your strength for defeating injustice and oppression in your steadfastness and prayers. Assuredly, God is on the side of the steadfast in truth.') Then the names of those members of the Meadow

Court families who were killed in the war or who remained missing were read out.

Ian, a church member and a former army bugler, had been given time off by his employers to sound the 'Last Post' and to break the two minutes' silence with the reveille. As he did so, a plane from Manchester airport flew overhead, and I remembered Adriana. Her name was not on the list, since she had not been killed by a bullet or a bomb. But she was a victim of the effects of war and, at that moment, her body was somewhere over Europe on its way home.

In the coming weeks, I was to return to the tree several times. Sometimes I found flowers placed around it, sometimes I saw a passer-by pause, when walking his dog, to read the plaque or simply to stand in silence. Fatos, the Kosovar boy who had shared in the planting of the tree, returned three months later with his father and uncle, Selatin and Safet, to expose the roots. Sylejman, Naim, my son David and I stood alongside as the two adults poured soil from the graves of their family members killed in a massacre in Kosova over the roots. It was a quiet and dignified moment, and when it was over, I shared with them some of the reasons why I had become so involved with the care of the Kosovar refugees.

Sylejman, who had clearly pondered what had motivated me, now asked why I had not told him before. I suppose that I had been looking for a suitable opportunity, and now it had arrived. The soil from the graves of those killed had disturbed our seemingly stable suburb and had linked us closer than ever to the reality of the Kosovar war.

7

Mission Impossible?

Blessed are the poor
  not the penniless, but those whose heart is free.
Blessed are those who mourn
  not those who whimper, but those who raise their
  voices.
Blessed are those who hunger and thirst for justice
  not those who whine, but those who struggle.
Blessed are the merciful
  not those who forget, but those who forgive.
Blessed are the pure in heart
  not those who act like angels, but those whose life is
  transparent.
Blessed are the peacemakers
  not those who shun conflict, but those who face it
  squarely.
Blessed are those who are persecuted for justice
  not because they suffer, but because they love.

P. Jacob of Santiago, Chile, included in *Liturgy of Life*,
an anthology compiled by Donald Hilton (NCEC 1991)

Three months after the war, the survivors of two families
arrived at Meadow Court. It was as though we had gone
back in time. Their look was familiar, their apprehension
palpable. One of the adults stood before me, his eyes fixed
on the interpreter who acted as his voice. Could I help him?

He needed to get his daughter out. He had not seen her since the war began and he was very anxious.

To make such an appeal to someone he had never met before meant, I reflected, that he must be either very trusting or very desperate. Probably both. For, as I had realized over the previous weeks, a person who is desperate will trust a complete stranger who is offering a welcoming hand. I had also come to realize that 'Mirë se vini Manchester, unë jam Bruce, si jeni?' ('Welcome to Manchester, I am Bruce, how are you?') was sufficient Albanian to show that I meant business. Few English people learn Albanian, and even my limited grasp would have amazed the teacher under whose guidance I failed French O level twice!

But who was this man? Where had he come from? Had he travelled alone? Why was his daughter not with him? Selatin, I discovered, had come to England with his brother Safet. Their wives, their mother, one of Selatin's children and two of Safet's, together with their sister and other family members, had been killed by Serb militia within three days of the NATO bombing campaign getting under way. The brothers had been working in Prishtina when the war began, and by the time they had returned home to Podujeva the massacre had already taken place.

I was to discover later that the women and children had been chased from garden to garden, tormented and lined up against a wall before the bullets were fired. Miraculously, four of Selatin's children had survived, but only one of Safet's. All but one of the children had travelled with them to Meadow Court. But where was nine-year-old Lirije? It appeared that, at first, neither Salatin nor Safet had any idea where she could be. She had not been buried with the other members of her family and she was not with her elder sister and two brothers. Only later had Selatin received a phone call from a family friend in Belgrade, revealing that Lirije was being 'cared for' in a hospital there. But how could she be discharged? The borders between Serbia and Kosova were closed and there were still claims, later confirmed, that many of the missing Kosovar Albanians were being held against their will in Serb camps. Why should the authorities bother with a little girl?

Selatin's plea demanded a response, and within minutes I had been persuaded. I was neither concerned by the size of the task nor deterred by the obstacles we were likely to face. Yes, we would hope and pray, but we would also do what we could. The best approach, I guessed, would probably be through the Serbian Orthodox Church. The Milošević regime would be unlikely to listen to a denomination with connections to the West. But the Orthodox Church, though to Albanian minds part of the basic problem – it had, after all, fostered Serb nationalism, on the one hand, and ignored the plight of persecuted people, on the other – could possibly provide effective channels of communication. I decided, therefore, that we would seek out the right contacts and make representations to the Orthodox. Selatin accepted that his appeal had been heard and that action would follow. All hope had not been lost. (He was later to tell me that, when all else is taken from you, hope remains – a conviction that was echoed by many, not just at Meadow Court.)

I made phone calls over the following days, but my efforts were redoubled after Safet showed me photographs of the family members he had lost. The pictures had been rescued after his possessions had been ransacked and, as a result, they were still splattered with mud. Apart from his brief explanations – 'my son', 'my wife', 'my daughter', 'my mother' – we looked in silence, the kind of deeply sympathetic silence of which I have already spoken, at these photographs of happy days, birthdays and festivals, days out and times at home. The children who had survived were pale and thin after their ordeal and visibly dazed by their new surroundings. But occasional smiles revealed the warmth and sincerity behind their sorrow, and despite their painful injuries they retained their dignity and poise.

To judge by the initial contacts which I had managed to make, negotiations with the Serbian Orthodox Church were going to be very tricky. Then the Chairman of my Methodist District revealed that he knew the Secretary of the European Council of Churches in Geneva. That was it! I would book an appointment, fly out to Geneva and beg him to speak to the representative of the Serbian Orthodox Church. Indeed, I even began to look ahead to the possibility of flying to Belgrade. I had no idea how I would get there, who I would see or what I would say, but I was preparing myself to go, and I shared my ideas with Selatin. He, for his part, was able to report that the Red Cross seemed to be making progress, and my plan was therefore placed on the back burner. I was disappointed and relieved in equal measure, but still willing, if need be, to make the journey.

A few weeks later, to our surprise and delight, Lirije crossed the border into Kosova and, on 4 November, flew into Leeds Bradford airport. It was the day before our Boys Brigade bonfire party at church. Many of the folk from Meadow Court joined us, and it was a happy night. We were concerned, at first, how people might be affected by the noise of the fireworks. But the shrieks of laughter and whoops of delight as explosion after explosion, flash after flash, filled the night sky quickly banished our fears. 'Is everything OK?', I had enquired, fearing that the noises could trigger painful memories. I need not have worried. One teenager replied, 'This is nothing. You should have heard the explosions in Kosova!'

Selatin's eyes were again fixed, not this time on the interpreter who acted as his voice, but on his daughter. Lirije stood before him, and I could see why someone somewhere had taken great pity on her. She was very beautiful and, despite the terrible wounds that had been inflicted on her, she was radiantly smiling at her doting father. Life was good – noisy and tiring, but good nevertheless.

Lirije, her sister and her cousin faced a series of complex operations. Jehona and Saranda's arms were very badly damaged by bullet wounds, and Lirije had been shot in the throat. Throughout her time in Belgrade, she had been fed directly into the stomach. At the bonfire party, she must have felt desperately frustrated not to be able to sample the generous supply of sweets and chocolates. But no frustration was evident – only the grace and poise characteristic of her family.

Shortly after her arrival, Lirije had received clothing vouchers to spend at a store in the Trafford Centre, a huge out-of-town shopping mall, not long opened and packed with the kind of goods that the Kosovars were unlikely ever to have seen. Naim had asked me to drive the family to the centre and, tired though I was, I was eager to do so. The other children wanted to look around the centre while Lirije, her father and Naim went to spend the vouchers, and it was agreed that all of us would meet at McDonald's at 8.00 p.m.

Christmas was just over a month away, and on that night tens of thousands of people were wandering about, in and out of shops crammed with everything imaginable. In the toy shop, which attracted the children like a magnet, the girls reached up simply to touch some Barbie dolls dressed as princesses. How many English girls of the same age, I asked myself, would be as thrilled to touch such objects? Few, I would imagine. But in possessing so much, I reflected, is not their capacity for delight dulled – and are not the designers denied the evidence which I saw of the impact their creations can produce? The girls' delight certainly captivated my heart, and I made a note of the dolls for future reference.

Eight o'clock soon rolled around and, after we had waited for ten minutes at McDonald's, Saranda looked at me and said, with what was then almost the full extent of her English, 'Mr Bruce, two McDonald's'. 'No', I replied, '8.00 p.m. at

McDonald's.' 'Yes, Mr Bruce, two McDonald's.' Then, pointing to the floor, 'McDonald's' and, pointing into the distance along the mall, 'Ship McDonald's'. Saranda, on her first trip to the Trafford Centre, knew more than I did. There are two McDonald's, a small one at the top end, where we were now anxiously seated, and a second, situated in a food hall that resembled the deck of an ocean liner. It was now well after 8.00 p.m., and we ran to the 'ship' McDonald's, only to find that the food hall – which, I am told, can hold 10,000 people – was almost filled to capacity.

I managed to find seats for the children, but my searches for Lirije, her father and Naim were to no avail. I kept returning to the girls who seemed to be becoming more and more concerned. My own anxiety was certainly increasing. Where were the others? What was I to do? Then, as I glanced across, Saranda beckoned me over. 'Mr Bruce, Mr Bruce,' she called. And, pulling a chair out with her good arm, gently pleaded in her best English, 'Please, sit down.' Temporarily losing even much-loved family members in the shopping centre of a big British city was nothing compared to what these children had faced just months earlier. I had a lot to learn, and the children had a wonderful way of teaching me!

In due course, the lost were found, and the journey back to Meadow Court was a happy one. I recall singing along to an Oasis track, appropriately titled 'Stand by Me', and even the news, a few days later, that Lirije had left her newly acquired clothes at the Trafford Centre elicited only a resigned sigh! But what Saranda had taught me about getting things into perspective was but the beginning of a longer and more radical process.

8

Heading for a Crisis

There is a pleasure in working with people in extreme situations; and a feeling of omnipotence that is close to despair: the carer wants to do more and more, and feels more and more helpless as a consequence ... Those who work with survivors are wary of identifying with the victim, of inflating their own capabilities and of the depression that comes when that illusion is pricked.

Neil Belton, *The Good Listener.*
Helen Bamber: A Life Against Cruelty
(Weidenfeld and Nicolson 1998), p. 151.

My responsibilities were beginning to prove too heavy, and I had panicked in the Trafford Centre. On reflection, such developments were entirely predictable. No one could have known, when I was at theological college in the 1980s, that I or any of my contemporaries would have to minister to survivors of war. And, in any case, ministerial training cannot be expected to cover every eventuality. Moreover, if the term 'ethnic cleansing' had already been coined in those days, we were not aware of it or of the reality to which it referred. A few more years had to pass and a quarter of a million people had to lose their lives in the Bosnian war before, sadly, it became a household phrase.

During those years, I sat, like so many others, before my television screen and watched with incredulity as the West's politicians, reluctant to respond to the humanitarian crises and acts of genocide in the break up of Yugoslavia, seemed to fudge the issues. On some occasions, I read about Srebrenica and felt utter frustration and shame; at other times, I put ethnic hatred and Balkan nationalism out of my mind and got on with my own life and work.

Croatia, Bosnia and Serbia, it must be acknowledged, seemed a long way away and I was not, I think, alone in failing to grasp that, just over two hours' flight from Manchester, people were being persecuted on a scale unprecedented in Europe since the Second World War.

Rwanda reawakened our consciences. Even so, what happened so quickly and so far away aroused in many only a shallow sympathy. After all, we convinced ourselves, there was little we could do about it. Those, however, with better understanding of the situation begged to differ, and in the light of what I have read and experienced since, I can only feel sorrow and shame that, merely fifty years after Auschwitz and the West's professed commitment to 'Never again!' we were prepared to fight for Kuwait's oil fields but not to challenge genocide.

The war in Kosova changed everything. It changed the lives of all who lived in that country's mountains and plains, its cities, towns and villages. It also changed, as Michael Ignatieff's outstanding book *Virtual War: Kosovo and Beyond*,[6] clearly indicates, how we fight wars and why.

The last century began with a war triggered by an assassination in Sarajevo and ended with another conflict in the same region. What, we may well ask, was learned during the intervening years? More effective methods of killing people or at least removing the enemy's 'mechanism for waging war' were certainly developed. Moreover, as the century progressed, the West became understandably more and more reluctant to commit its forces to battle, and thus to risk losing its youth. Between 1914 and 1918 almost an entire generation was lost but in Kosova, though there were 10,000 other casualties, not a single NATO soldier was killed in action. In between, many lives were lost in many wars, and perhaps there had been a growing realization that every life is precious and that no life should be lost irresponsibly. 'Enough is enough' is a noble thought and, for me, who belongs to a generation that has never experienced conscription, one that is easy to express. But as I watched the first news reports of ethnic cleansing in Kosova, it seemed a self-evident truth.

Shortly after Meadow Court received its first residents, not only the bombing campaign but also the provision being made for Kosovar refugees began to be questioned. One person even dared to suggest that, in the long term, ethnic cleansing was probably the best solution, on the grounds that, if the various ethnic groups were each located in their own territory, peace and stability would follow. This completely and utterly horrified me. So far as I could see, to force entire peoples across borders could only destabilize the region yet further, and risked plunging the world, not just Europe, into an even bigger war. It also implied that, if rioting broke out in an inner city, the police force should abandon the area, for Kosova was a riot on a massive scale. An entire people was being persecuted and forced from their homes. Villages were being looted and set ablaze. Women were being raped and children killed. And all the while we in the West were planning our summer holidays.

The only way in which some holidaymakers were affected by such crimes against humanity was that Croatia was temporarily removed from their list of possible destinations. 'Never again!' Never again what? Never again consider the cost of confronting the crimes of nationalism and genocide? Never again commit ourselves to saying 'No' to dictators and oppression? If armies are used to wage wars of economic and territorial gain, I cannot support them. But if they are used to

protect people from those who would persecute, rape, maim
and kill them, I can only admire the self-sacrifice involved. After
all, I have never been required to risk my life for people I have
never met and, culturally, have little in common with; and I
find it difficult to know how I would react if I was. But some
of those who benefited from NATO's action were finding
their feet less than a mile from my home and I was compelled
to wrestle with these issues as never before.

In the days following the first flight carrying Kosovan refugees to Manchester, it seemed that we could not put a foot
wrong. To follow the directive of Jesus, 'Ask and it will be
given to you; seek and you will find; knock and the door will
be opened to you', was no difficult task. We had sought a
place where refuge could be provided, and there it stood,
along a lane that I had not previously known existed. We
had asked for many things and, more often than not, they
were quickly and willingly given. We had even knocked on
many doors, and few were slammed in our faces. It surely
could not last. And it didn't. I guess that my exhaustion
covered up some of the warning signs. Had I not been so
busy, or so obsessed with it all, I might have been more
prepared. In the event, however, I wasn't prepared.

In the period after Christmas, as I sought to recover from
the crisis described in the next chapter, I read Neil Belton's
wonderful biography of Helen Bamber. My wife had bought
it for me, thinking that it was solely concerned with work
alongside Holocaust survivors, and that I would find it of
interest. In the event, it provided much more than she antici-
pated: both important information and invaluable help in
getting my personal situation into perspective. The passage
which stands at the head of this chapter was especially
enlightening, not least in its reference to the depression which
comes when illusion is pricked.

My own illusions were about to be pricked, my bubble was
about to burst, and, looking back, maybe God took a hand

in what happened. But first I had to allow the bubble to grow so large that, eventually and inevitably, it would come into contact with God's pin.

9

A Valley and a Vision

O Lord, you have searched me and you know me.
You know when I sit and when I rise;
you perceive my thoughts from afar.
You discern my going out and my lying down;
you are familiar with all my ways.

If I say 'Surely the darkness will hide me
and the light become night around me',
even the darkness will not be dark to you;
the night will shine like the day,
for darkness is as light to you.

For you created my inmost being;
you knit me together in my mother's womb.

Psalm 139

The work at Meadow Court had gone wonderfully well in the first seven months, and we were about to celebrate our first Christmas together. The local Methodist churches had taken responsibility for the purchase of presents and, recognizing the need to avoid disparity, we had suggested a suitable figure and hoped for one present per person. We did not dare to expect anything more. In the event, however, despite the media having changed the focus of their attention, people were exceedingly generous, and at least one sack per family was loaded onto Santa's sleigh, a milk float commandeered for Christmas Eve. I should have been delighted. But, as I wandered round the communal lounge, firing off photographs of the excited crowd, I felt dazed and unable to take in what was happening.

A few days earlier, to be sure, a problem had reared its head. A few of the men at Meadow Court had been informed that, in a programme known as 'Explore and Prepare', they would be returning to Kosova at a few hours' notice. The idea was that a selected member of each family would be flown to Kosova to make arrangements for the others to return there at a later date. Whilst each person on the programme had volunteered, they had no idea at the beginning that they would have leave at such short notice or that they would not know how soon they could be reunited with their families. Banush, who had set himself the task of learning English but had found his time consumed by looking after his young family and his paralysed brother, bade me farewell and, with immense concentration, called after me, 'Mr Bruce . . . Happy Christmas'. Ylber, as he left, dismissed the problem with typical aplomb: 'Last time, we had only ten minutes to leave, and this time we do not have a gun at our backs.' But I was furious and expressed my disquiet in a letter to the British Refugee Council. A few days later, I was relieved to receive a phone call, indicating that, after a high-level meeting at the Home Office at which my letter had been circulated, there would be changes in the programme.

This episode, then, could not be blamed for my unhappy state. Indeed, everything that I can remember of that Christmas Eve should have brought me joy. Dylber, younger brother of Ylber and now, at seventeen, acting head of the family in his absence, appeared before me, having paid a visit to the off-licence in the pouring rain, and presented me with a bottle of wine. 'Happy Christmas, Mr Bruce', he said, and I will never forget his impulsive act of appreciation. And many others crowded round, thrusting hand after hand into mine and planting kiss after kiss on my cheeks. It all constituted an affirmation of what I had tried to do, and it should have buoyed me up like the cry of 'They are worthy' in the Ordination Service. But, at that moment, I felt anything but worthy.

Why? During the previous weeks, I had begun to expect the unexpected and to believe in the unbelievable. I had grown beyond confidence into something altogether more sinister. What I wanted to happen would happen. What we needed for Meadow Court and my Kosovar friends would be obtained somehow from somewhere. There were no doubts whatsoever – we were winning, and disappointment and defeat never entered my head. What had begun as wholehearted commitment to a worthy cause had developed into a self-assurance that bordered on sheer arrogance.

My new-found belief in realizing the impossible did not find expression at Meadow Court alone. Thanks to this new 'spirit' within me, I could not believe that anything or anyone was beyond my reach. But this delusion could not be allowed to persist. I was neither equipped nor called to go beyond what God intended for me.

Others, I know, will have realized this before I did. But it came home to me as I sat in my garage in the dark. As a child, I had detested the dark, and when, as a teenager, I had worked in a bakery on the night shift, I had valued the camaraderie but shrunk from night work as from something unnatural. But now the darkness seemed almost comforting. Would it be a happy release from the pressures I was under? In the past, I had sometimes thought that those who committed suicide must have been very courageous. But what I was considering in that brief, irrational moment would have been the easy option. To go on was much harder. The sounds of my sons' voices brought me back. The day was ahead, but how would I get through it?

A phone call to Bill, a minister I had only met twice before, consolidated my hold on reality. I was later to discover that

Fridays were his day off, and that normally he would not even have answered the phone. However, on that particular day, for some unknown reason, he did – and thank God he did. He taught me a great deal by what he said and did not say, by his grace and generosity, by his wisdom and understanding. He gave me the confidence to get through the day.

That day, however, was but the beginning of a long process of reflection about my life. For I needed to understand both why, as it seemed to me, my previous experience had been a preparation for the work with the Kosovars and also why the task had overwhelmed me.

My own experience of deprivation, I decided, fuelled a ready sympathy within me for anyone in need. My natural father died suddenly at the age of twenty-three, just two months after my conception. My grandmother, who cared for me in my earliest years, died when I was four years old. When my mother remarried, I found myself with a step-brother and stepsisters much older than myself, and I longed, in vain, for a playmate of my own age. My grandfather, who had been a surrogate father to me, died when I had completed two and a half years' training as a civil engineer.

My own experience, then, enabled me to appreciate how bereaved, lonely, frustrated people feel. But what more than sympathy could I offer them? Was there anything that was offered to me that I could pass on?

Within my stepfamily, my desire for my own brother or sister to love and to be loved by grew and grew, and I wanted to know how it could be fulfilled. Apparently, baby brothers and sisters were very expensive, costing lots of pennies. Undeterred, I managed to secrete any money given to me, and hoarded it in my treasure box (an old Clark's shoe box, huge in my estimation, but probably the original packaging of shoes to fit my own four-year-old feet). Then, when I felt that the sum contained in the box was vast, I took it from under my bed and carried it to the corner shop. I looked up, beyond the metal advertising boards covering the bottle-green counter, to the silver-haired lady. I learned that, sadly, there were no baby brothers or sisters in stock, but the man with a van would come on Friday and she would ask him.

As time went by, it dawned on me that no baby brother or sister was going to arrive. But, thankfully, I had met an angel. The shopkeeper, Mrs Clara Angell, was so touched by my request and my subsequent calls and conversations that she wondered if I would like to call her 'Auntie Angell'. In this way, she became in effect a replacement grandmother.

Auntie Angell was the obvious choice to take me to church. My stepsiblings were making their way through puberty and adolescence, and a four-year-old would have cramped their style. Thanks, therefore, to an old, childless shopkeeper who understood my desire and took pity on me, my lifelong commitment to the Methodist Church began. Almost without realizing it, I grasped the importance of discerning the need of a neighbour, no matter how young they might be, and being willing to stand alongside them. And I have much more than that for which to thank my angel, my Auntie Angell.

It is extraordinary that, in the first instance, she was responsible for taking me to church, and that, in later years, I gladly helped her to get there. She was thus able to attend the last service I conducted before entering theological college, and I cherish a vivid memory of an old lady giggling as she was carried up the stairs by four men, one on each limb, for the post-service bun fight!

In the weeks following my grandfather's death, I went for many walks and, on one such occasion, I had an encounter that would change the course of my life.

The day began with a touch of farce. I hate waiting around in barber's shops. I have always preferred to be first in the queue. George Rose's barber's shop was due to open at 8.00 a.m., and I took my place outside at 7.25. Such was

George's popularity that by 7.55 there were five or six others in the queue. 'He's late today,' announced the man next to me. 'Yes, he's usually here by now,' commented the third in line. 'Looks well if he's gone on holiday!' laughed the man next to me. I turned to read the notice, till then undetected, in the doorway. As I skulked away, covered in embarrassment, I was just able to say, 'I'm afraid he has'.

I found myself wandering over Shoal Hill, a part of Cannock Chase well known to me, since as a child I had explored it with my maternal grandfather. Suddenly, I felt compelled to stop and turn, and as I did so, I was overcome by a sense of awe. There, right before me was a Presence that I can only describe as Peace. No words were addressed to me. Indeed, nothing needed to be said. I recall that, as I stood in silence, I felt that the Presence was drawing into me and that I was being drawn into the Presence. I also recall wanting the moment to last for ever. But it didn't, and I went on my way, wondering what the experience meant and where it would lead.

As the months went by, I became ever more aware of the need to put my life in order. The period immediately before and immediately after my grandfather's death had passed in a haze. I guess I was a typical teenager exploring adulthood and feeling very much alone. My grandfather had always been concerned about me and from the moment that, with other members of the youth group, I began to share in services he must have realized that the time could come when I would consider entering the ministry. Indeed, only a fortnight before he died, he enquired about my future plans. He had not pressured me to take up civil engineering, but the fact that he was himself a civil engineer and had taken me to see projects in which he had been involved must clearly have influenced me. Then one night I glimpsed my grandfather, in light and in peace; and he simply said, 'Do it'. I was sure that I knew exactly what he meant. And when, next day, my minister felt compelled to ask me if I had ever considered offering for the ministry, my conviction was confirmed.

But now, twenty years later, the practice of that same ministry had forced me to face fundamental questions about myself and my faith. Why was I doing all this for the folk at Meadow Court? Who had given me the right to do it? Was it about God? Or was it about me? Was it about loving others unconditionally, or acquiring something previously denied me? Was it about exercising faith, or facing my past? For whom was I exercising this ministry? God? A people in dire need? Or myself?

I needed more than reassurance about a commission received long ago, more than the confidence produced by a phone call with someone far away, more even than the love of someone near at hand. As the new millennium was about to dawn, I needed to be honest with God about my past, including my recent past, and to seek strength from him to face the future.

A few days after Christmas, we took a trip as a family to my old haunt of Lichfield. It was a cold morning and, as we stepped out of the car, we discovered that the tarmac was iced over. I nearly lost my balance, but my determination to stay on my feet and reach my destination was itself an acted parable!

It had been in Lichfield that, as a twenty-year-old, I had relished youthfulness in a wine bar and pondered eternity in the Cathedral Close. Now I ascended the ancient steps that led to the chapel set aside for private prayer. The climb seemed to drain what little energy was left in me. But deep down I was desperately determined to seek, there and then in that place of prayer, the help that only God could give.

The sign 'Silence – Private Prayer' seemed ineffective. Two people, huddled together, were praying out loud at the far end. I could hear them before I entered the chapel. But I was not to be deterred and, sitting down, I slowly closed my eyes.

As my body relaxed, the sound of those vocal prayers seemed to diminish. Surprised, I opened my eyes to see what was happening. The couple must have been praying as loudly as ever, but now I no longer heard them. As my eyes closed again, I was unaware of time and space but conscious of being in the presence of God. And I begged him to forgive me and to strengthen me to go on. I cannot explain or even describe what followed. But I received an assurance that I was forgiven and that there was a future to be entered. As I became aware, once more, of where I was, the sound of the jargon-filled prayers continued unabated. I hope that, if they were as desperately offered as mine, they may have been as wonderfully answered.

Exhaustion, whether it be self-inflicted or the product of heartfelt obedience to a call of God, can damage your health, and full recovery is rarely swift. In my case, my answered prayer was quickly followed by flu, and I spent three weeks lounging around, still regretting my past mistakes but also being reassured that God could still make use of me, weak and vulnerable though I am.

Meadow Court had only been open for eight months, and little did I know that it was to remain open for a further fourteen months. What I did know, however, was that I would be there for as long as it took. I would have to be more realistic and responsible in the future, but I would be there.

IO

A Never-ending Conclusion

Looking for the Way

In the month of Elul when men prepare their souls for the days of judgement, Rabbi Hayyim was in the habit of telling stories to a tune that moved all his listeners to turn to God. Once he told this story: 'A man lost his way in a great forest. After a while another lost his way and chanced on the first. Without knowing what had happened to him, he asked the way out of the woods. "I don't know," said the first. "But I can point out the ways that lead further into the thicket, and after that let us try to find the way together."'

'So, my congregation', the rabbi concluded his story, 'let us look for the way together.'

Martin Buber, *Tales of the Hasidim*
(Shocken Books Inc. 1975)

Following my experience in the chapel set aside for private prayer in Lichfield Cathedral, I turned again to daily devotions. In the busyness of the preceding months, my prayer life had somehow been squeezed out. I could say that I now acknowledged a need to reacquaint myself with my initial source of inspiration. But it is probably more accurate to say that I responded to the One who was calling me back.

The Psalms, in particular, spoke to me as never before.

Their understanding of exodus and wilderness, of exile and of the sustaining hope of return became meaningful in an entirely new way. So too did the command to love and care for our neighbours, be they strangers or even our enemies. I felt, in fact, something of the impact that the parable of the good Samaritan must have made on its first hearers. To them the picture of a hated Samaritan risking his life and engaging in considerable expense to care for a Jew must have come as a terrible shock. Small wonder that, to prevent the parable from disturbing our own cosy existence, we treat it as a nice story about helping others.

In my case, however, there can be no doubt that helping the Kosovars who came to Meadow Court had as great an impact as the parable itself. As I have tried to explain, it was not an isolated experience, and its significance lay in its relationship to all that had happened to me previously. It changed my life – not in a single moment, but over a period of time.

When, for example, Shpresa put her fair and honest question, 'Why do you do this for my people?', just three weeks after the first flight, I was not ready to answer. Behind the question put by a local churchgoer, 'Who gave you the right to do this?', I sensed a legalism at odds with the expression of love. At the same time, I had no doubt that we were obeying Christ's command and that, sooner or later, our actions would speak for themselves.

I was coming to realize, however, how many factors hamper the sustained expression of a truly loving concern. The media, for example, diverted attention elsewhere, and shifts in language – soon after the war ended, the refugees were renamed 'evacuees' – indicated a change in the Government's assessment of priorities. Moreover, a television documentary looked at a centre housing dispersed asylum-seekers, many of whom had fled Kosova. The response of the local community had been appalling. 'Not in my back yard' was the prevailing attitude. No one from the neighbourhood had visited but, it was reported, a man who walked his dog occasionally waved. A shot of an asylum-seeker walking past a church with a sign advertising a coffee morning for Kosova was particularly disturbing. The documentary team did not draw attention to this, and perhaps they did not notice it. But I did. It seems that, though we are often good at raising money to be sent to worthy causes, caring for those on our doorstep is too much to ask. It seems too that when we pray for an end to oppression and racial tension we tacitly assume that the transformation of our world will occur elsewhere and be undertaken by someone else.

Again, we reveal an insatiable appetite for novels and films about the Holocaust and, perhaps to cover our own guilt and shame, idolize those who helped the victims of Nazi persecution. But we fail to recognize that many, reaching our ports on the backs of lorries, are fleeing from similar oppression and are in desperate need of similar support. In short, the well-known photograph of a couple sunbathing on a Mediterranean beach just yards from the body of an asylum-seeker washed up by the last tide symbolizes a pervasive indifference and an occasional hostility towards our neighbours in need.

The situation is compounded by two other negative attitudes. First, tribalism. We read what our Scriptures have to say about justice and harmony and are moved by Jesus weeping over Jerusalem and exclaiming, 'If only you knew the things that make for peace.' But we do not reflect about today's cities where, though there are people of many faiths and perspectives, few venture out of their own camp. Christians, indeed, may compare the number of Muslims with those who attend Christian worship and feel threatened. They may also fail to recognize that their own faith has its roots in Judaism and that Jesus himself was a Jew. As a consequence, defensiveness results in isolation and ignorance produces narrowness of vision. How, in such a situation, can peace be realized or sustained?

Second, imperialism. It is all too easy to assume, as our forebears tended to do, that, when everyone else becomes like us and behaves like us, peace will come. But the path to peace can only begin from where we are, not from where we were. Too much has happened in recent decades and too many people have moved from where they were, physically, intellectually and spiritually, for progress to be made without entering into dialogue with those who are different from us and who offer new ways of looking at our world.

Perhaps we must begin, then, by addressing the tensions that exist without our own local churches. It seems to me that the greatest tension of all is between the old and the new, between the traditional and the innovative. Such a division may always have existed in some form, but it is particularly clearcut today. It is extraordinary, however, that some who are eager to move the church forward in her worshipping style are reluctant to explore the tremendously liberating theological developments of recent times. They often seem reluctant, in fact, to seek understanding beyond the pages of the Bible and, even in Scripture, are very selective about the verses that matter! Is there nothing to be learnt, then, from all that has happened and all that has been written since the books of the New Testament were produced and assembled?

To delve into the latest insights, deriving from archaeological discoveries, biblical and theological explorations and dialogue with other disciplines, is a daunting task. However, as I began to ponder and respond to God's call to ministry, one minister offered me this advice: 'It is better to dig deep into a dark mine and find a tiny diamond, than to stay on the surface.' I often recall those books that were given to me by the widow of a Methodist local preacher as I was about to enter theological college. Her late husband had worked at the local coal mine and the books that he had read were filled with his handwritten notes. If only all of those who entered our pulpits today were as serious about study. It is frightening that so many opt for literature which backs up a well-honed faith rather than for books which would lead them into new territory.

It seems to me that Jesus was happier with the humble than with the proud, with those who were uncertain but honest than with those who were confident but unreflective, with those who had questions than with those who thought they had all the answers. I am convinced, therefore, that the time has come for us to be bold both in our search and our speaking, in our reflecting and our rejoicing, in our worship and in our work as followers of Jesus. We are called to celebrate grace and not to be bound by rigid preconceptions. Changing the world into the one that God has in mind is a tall order, but the world changes in me the moment I address my own fears and intolerance and care for my neighbour in need, especially when that neighbour is of a different culture or faith.

It may be, however, that some will be worried about this approach. They will be concerned, in fact, that I may be throwing out the baby with the bathwater. They may fear that the faith which results will be unrecognizable as in any sense Christian. I hope that what follows will dispel such anxieties.

In the spring of 2000, twelve months after Meadow Court opened, I read of Cassie Bernall, who was one of the teenage pupils killed in the Columbine High School massacre on 20 April 1999.[7] Cassie had, after a turbulent time in her life, committed herself to Christ and was prepared to say 'Yes' when her killer pointed the gun at her head and asked if she believed in God. Reports of the incident were having a profound effect on young people and parents alike, and I decided to hold an evening for the teenagers at church. My aim was to provide an opportunity for them to view the video of an interview with Cassie's parents and to learn more of the background to what was becoming seen as modern-day martyrdom.

As the teenagers from Meadow Court were now attending our weekly Youth Fellowship, they would have to be invited to the evening. There were matters, however, which demanded careful thought. First, the film would feature a massacre that had taken place at the time that they themselves were fleeing ethnic cleansing – indeed, some of those present would have survived a massacre. Second, the presentation and indeed the whole evening would constitute a Christian event, in the sense that Cassie had been inspired by Christian faith and anything that I said would be from the same perspective. I spoke to each of the families at Meadow Court and without exception they were happy for their teenagers to be present and to participate as fully as they wished. In my conversation with Sylejman, I explained that what I was about to do, like everything that I had done so far, was rooted in my faith, my belief in Jesus, his life and teaching. Sylejman's response stunned me: 'You don't have to tell us these things – we know it to be true because we see it with our own eyes.'

To encounter people on their own territory and to meet their needs without any motive other than love is to express faith in a clear and unambiguous way. But all too often, in our insecurity, we speak hastily about our beliefs and our direct language builds barricades rather than bridges. As a result, suspicion and mistrust follow, and sadly the end product is hostility and silence.

Fortunately, things worked out very differently at Meadow Court, not least because actions did speak louder than words, and also paved the way for words. When I met with the interpreters for a meal in the summer of 1999, we were wrong in assuming that the work at Meadow Court would only last for a year but right in thinking that its impact, on us and on others, would affect the rest of our lives. As I see my friends

Remzi and Banush master English and we engage in ever deeper topics of conversation; as I watch Sylejman play with his new granddaughter; as I hear Sadri describe his joy in being involved with a local handball team; as I observe Selatin and Safet's obvious pride in their children; and as I visit each home and find not only a welcome but a rich peace, I know that it has been worth every ounce of energy, every sleepless night, every tear shed. The past will always be there and will often haunt us: memories of parents and siblings who were killed, of homes and friends that were lost, and of a land that seems so far away will always be lurking. But there is also a future up ahead, and my prayer is that my friends will carry into it something of the faith, hope and love that pervaded Meadow Court.

But what about me? It has been an emotional experience to look back, to record the events of those days and to reflect upon them. Others who were present at the time will remember what happened differently, but I can only write from my own perspective, and if you have been able to feel something of what I felt and to perceive something of what I was able to perceive, I am content.

What I have come to understand as never before is the nature of discipleship. To follow Jesus is to learn from him, and what we most need to learn is how to love our neighbours, recognizing that they too are God's creatures, made in his image. As disciples, then, we should stand alongside those who grieve and those who rejoice, sharing both their despair and their hopes and being willing not only to shoulder their burdens but to allow them to shoulder ours. There is much that we can give to people of other races and cultures, and much that we can receive from them. For the diversity of human life, far from being dangerous and divisive, can enrich life together on this tiny planet.

We sometimes ponder what Jesus would say and do if he were to return. Some believe that he would exercise sovereign power, rewarding the godly and punishing the wicked. Perhaps, however, he would continue to ask the kind of probing questions which characterized his previous ministry. Some questions could well be about historical events. Why, he might ask, were six million Jews rounded up, transported, selected and killed by, in the main, baptized Christians? And why was the Serbian Orthodox Church silent as 'Muslims', the majority of whom were non-practising and therefore offered no religious threat, were persecuted and sent packing? Why indeed did no pope visit a mosque until John Paul II did so – in Damascus! – on 6 May 2001?

Other questions could be more personal and therefore more uncomfortable. Why, for example, are our personal ambitions and private agendas more important to us than God's ambitions for the world and the agenda presented by those who have glimpsed his goals? Why do we criticize and condemn those within our own faith community who have a different theological perspective? Why do so many believe that it is important to have all the answers and that they possess them? Why do we not love each other as God loves us?

Our world is shrinking at an alarming rate. A century ago our neighbours were of the same village or street, and in the main they shared our heritage and faith. Today our neighbours may be from any country in the world and are unlikely to share our history or beliefs. Even though our hopes and dreams for a fairer and brighter future for those whom we love and ought to love may be the same, our values and convictions may come from very different spiritual roots. Perhaps in this new century ecumenism should be inter-faith rather than inter-denominational.

In saying this, I do not wish to give the wrong impression. For my own faith in the uniqueness of Jesus as God's son, in his teaching as truth, and in the overcoming of the darkness of death by his resurrection, far from being diminished has been greatly strengthened by my recent experiences. What has changed is my overall appreciation of the historical and cultural context in which my faith must be held and practised. And the new insights have both informed and inspired me.

The late Hugo Gryn, Holocaust survivor and popular rabbi, stated in his last speech that future historians would consider the twentieth century as marked by refugees as well as by two world wars.[8] We are now beginning to realize how right he was. We accept that more and more people are likely to seek refuge, if not from warfare, then from oppression, poverty, environmental disaster and disease. They will bring with them new challenges for us, from their culture, their religious traditions and their experience.

How we respond will depend upon our faith. Is it confident and open enough to love without thought of cost or recompense? Is it brave enough to receive as well as to give? Is it true to the gospel that brings good news to the poor, release to the captives, recovery of sight to the blind and liberty to the oppressed? If it is, then perhaps as we stand before our maker we may hear the words, 'Inasmuch as you did this for one of the least among you, you did it for me.'

At the end of the Cassie Bernall video presentation, I challenged all of the teenagers to consider staying behind to commit themselves to finding out more about the God who had inspired Cassie to stand before her killer with such confidence. Those from Meadow Court far outnumbered the teenagers from church. It was a moving moment, complemented by a remark on the following morning. Petrit, who has popped up on these pages just as he pops up in real life, said, 'All for God, Mr Bruce, all for God.' I could not help thinking that he was commenting on more than the night before.

Kosovar Responses

11

24,000 Hours in a Day –
A Poem about War and Hope

Staff and volunteers at Blessed Thomas Holford R C Secondary School were wonderfully helpful to the teenagers of Meadow Court. They were concerned not only to assist their academic development but also to support them as they began to come to terms with the horrors they had faced.

One poem, reproduced here, seems to express vividly the stark reality of the youngsters' sense of loss and of their fears. Written, with help from others, by four of the teenagers – Adonis Alaj, Fatos Bogujevci, Petrit Hashani and Adrian Hoxha – it was later included on a compilation CD sold to help victims of war (Cohesion, Manchester Aid to Kosovo).

Before the War

Before the war the clouds were grey
Because things were still forbidden
Our schools had been taken away
We had to keep them hidden

Friendships breaking
Looking for help
Unhappiness
Bombs
Nights without sleep
Nightmares

Trying to keep our language
Tension
Stress

During the War

I saw a child who could not play
That was all he really wanted
Those long, long days, little food, no water, just dismay.
Kindness, not cruelty, only that was needed.

Hope
Endless war
Fear
NATO
Our saviour.

Thanks for being alive
Cruelty and kindness
Days without food
Protect the little ones
Who had no chance to play.

After the War

It's strange to feel happy and yet feel sad
For we lost so many friends
Together we'll advance – feel glad
That hope – it never ends

Teachers killed in Kosova
Solidarity
Happy but sad
Good friends
Good teachers
A 14 year-old boy especially remembered
Thanks to Britain
Together, we'll move forward in peace, for ever.
Together, we'll move forward in peace, for ever.

12

Testimonies from Four Kosovar Families

It is not enough, I am absolutely sure, simply to acknowledge the warm support and encouragement which the Kosovars have given me in the writing of this book. Readers must be given the chance to hear them speak for themselves, both telling of their experiences and expressing their views of the venture centred on Meadow Court. What follows is offered as a representative selection of responses from:

Sylejman, who met with me early on, while still suffering from the beating he had received from Serb paramilitaries, to discuss the way ahead;

Remzi, who, though paralysed for many years and unable to leave his bed, taught himself almost perfect English;

Amir, who is now back home in Kosova, married and planning a family;

Saranda, who at sixteen has survived some of the worst that human beings can do to each other.

They speak for their families, and family trees are therefore included for the reader's guidance.

Their words need no comment from me.

Family trees

The Alaj/Ferizi family

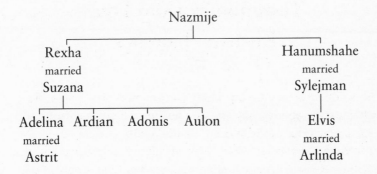

Nazmije

Rexha
married
Suzana

Hanumshahe
married
Sylejman

Adelina   Ardian   Adonis   Aulon
married
Astrit

Elvis
married
Arlinda

The Bogujevci family

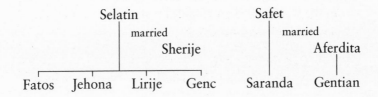

Selatin
married
Sherije

Safet
married
Aferdita

Fatos   Jehona   Lirije   Genc

Saranda   Gentian

The Gashi family

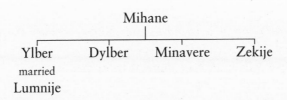

Mihane

Ylber   Dylber   Minavere   Zekije
married
Lumnije

The Hashani family

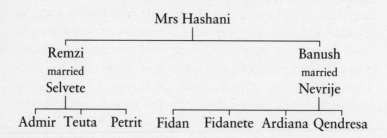

Mrs Hashani

Remzi
married
Selvete

Banush
married
Nevrije

Admir Teuta Petrit   Fidan   Fidanete Ardiana Qendresa

The Hoxha family

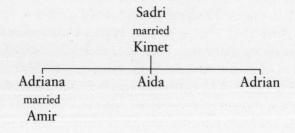

Sadri
married
Kimet

Adriana   Aida   Adrian
married
Amir

The Lamaxhema family

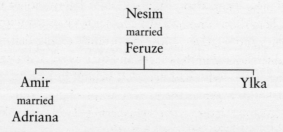

Nesim
married
Feruze

Amir   Ylka
married
Adriana

Syljeman Ferizi

I wouldn't have left my beloved country unless the lives of all those trapped in my flat had been in danger. The paramilitary force of Serbian police made their way from Serbia to Kosova with no other purpose than to massacre my innocent and defenceless people. They applied relentless pressure, making our circumstances more and more difficult and eventually forcing us to flee from Prishtina.

When we left, to tell the truth, we weren't sure that we would be able to escape from their barbaric hands. For the Voice of America told us on 29 April 1999 that 700,000 Albanians had left Kosova. It also reported that the Serbian operations in the villages had been completed and that the towns would now be cleared. In such a situation, any attempt to leave was clearly dangerous. But my mother-in-law was very ill and needed hospital treatment. To get her to Skopje hospital we paid a large sum in foreign currency and left Kosova on the same day. After eleven days in Macedonia, we set out for Great Britain on the evening of 11 May 1999.

Our welcome at Manchester airport was unbelievable and contrasted strongly with our experiences on our journey from Skopje. The Macedonian aviation staff treated us offensively, not removing their masks when doing official assessments. The friendly English people, on the other hand, not only received us warmly but provided a splendid dinner with a range of different meat courses, refreshing drinks and many other things. They also organized eight international phone lines to help those who had lost contact for months with their loved ones and relatives. Most importantly of all, their honest hospitality showed in their faces and they expressed a genuine interest in those who had been left behind in Kosova and in all that had happened there. Not surprisingly, some of the oldest Kosovar ladies were whispering 'God has taken us from hell and brought us to paradise'.

All one hundred and forty-six Kosovars who reached GB on 12 May 1999 were placed in two reception centres in the Trafford Borough. Those who needed medical treatment were immediately transferred to hospital in Manchester. The rest were taken to their accommodation, and I, my in-laws and some others were placed at Meadow Court in Altrincham, where we stayed for 21 months and 3 days.

We were treated like any other residents of that area and cannot speak too highly of the help that we received. We were respected and supported in every possible way, both financially and with amusements and recreations. The fact that we were enabled to watch Albanian and later Kosovar TV by satellite was especially appreciated. We were also helped by two religious groups united in their humanitarian concern – and I recall, as if it were yesterday, our interpreter, Naim Korenica, announcing that the minister of the Methodist Church in Timperley and a woman from the Altrincham Muslim Association had come together to see me. We also appreciated the English language classes and the art classes which were arranged for us.

What all Kosovar refugees will remember most warmly, however, is the contribution of the Methodist Church under the leadership of their minister Bruce Thompson. The teenagers in particular appreciated the excursions round central England, the visits to Manchester United, the use of the local Sports Centre (for swimming and other sports), the free seats at Altrincham FC and the football tournaments which were arranged; and the young children – for example, Fidan Hashani, Genc Bogujevci, Adrian Hoxha, Adonis Alaj, Petrit Hashani, Dylber Gashi, Fatos Bogujevci and Anest Gjini – felt that their interests were fully appreciated. Moreover, the fourteen Kosovars who returned home were assisted financially with a very generous gift.

The Methodists from Timperley were largely responsible for opening and equipping the Meadow Court Centre and for the first ten days provided and prepared the food for free. And they continued to support the Kosovars when other helpers faded away. In particular, they showed deep concern for the Hoxha family after the tragic death of their daughter Adriana. And the seriousness of their interest was sealed by Bruce Thompson's visit to Kosova in July 2001.

I could have written more, but I think that others will want to express their own appreciation in this book which Bruce Thompson is preparing. I personally want to wish him and his family joy in the future and success in this project. God bless you, Mr Bruce, for you have shown yourself to be a good man and a rare friend to the Albanians who found shelter in this place. As our friend, you took the initiative to plant the life tree and set up the plaque which commemorates those massacred in Kosova; and what you did will never be forgotten in the Albanian history which has still to be written.

Once again, thank you very much.

Remzi Hashani

During the flight to Great Britain, I kept asking myself whether I had made the right decision. Would it have been better to stay in the refugee camp until the war was over? But despite the intervention of the international community, the war continued and I had no hope, at that moment, that it would end so soon.

For me, coming to GB was a journey into the unknown. But I firmly believed that there must be a better world than the one I was leaving behind. Moreover, my concern for the safety of my family and my own urgent need of medical treatment pointed to evacuation as our best course. And it happened so quickly that I wasn't really prepared for it. Only a month before, I had been lying in a cold cellar trying to survive and thinking that we could be killed or starved or die from cold. At that point, the possibility of leaving

Kosova seemed unreal and quite beyond anything that I could achieve. But life can be full of surprises, especially during a war.

In the refugee camp, as people stood outside the GB office waiting to be identified, their eyes were lifeless and they talked very quietly. They appeared to me to be people who were lost and without hope. And when we reached Britain, we were exhausted, physically and psychologically. The traumas of the war affected everybody, especially children and the elderly, and many people were sick or injured. But in Meadow Court people began to get their confidence back and to look very different. Most importantly, health improved and there were many signs that people were feeling better. Smiles returned to children's faces and they began to forget the past and look to the future.

On that first day at Meadow Court in the Spring of 1999, there was a lot of beautiful sunshine. As I lay in bed, I could both see lots of greenery through the window and hear many voices, inside and outside the building. English and Albanian were being spoken as people were getting to know one another. As children played in the park, lots of local people came and went. Some brought clothes and toys for the children, others enquired what we needed. I remember my brother's daughter, Fidaneta, rushing in to say that she had a bicycle. I asked her whether she could ride one. 'Yes!' was the joyful reply, as she dashed out again. Mr Bruce Thompson, minister of the local Methodist church, had arranged for dinner to be prepared by local women volunteers, and the welcome was beyond my expectations. In a word, it was 'wonderful'! We felt in the midst of friends.

In the following days, visits were arranged to the city of Manchester and its suburbs and to Manchester United FC, and all our basic needs were met. Ten days after we arrived at Meadow Court, I felt strong enough to go outside in a wheelchair, and this became my daily routine. I was able to look at the green landscape, to watch the children playing in the park, and to meet and chat with local people.

One day, standing near the main gate, I met the author of this book, Mr Bruce, for the first time. I was curious to meet him because my brother spoke well of him. He approached me and introduced himself. I could speak only a few words in English, but I understood him, and there was an interpreter if I needed help. In the following months, it felt as though Mr Bruce was a member of each family. He helped us with our problems and attended any social events, most of which he arranged.

After a month, the war ended. The news made everyone happy. We all had friends, close relatives or other members of our family circle in Kosova, and though we were living here, our minds were there. But we had been unable to get in touch with any of them, and we only learned later that Sylejman's two brothers had been killed during the war.

The summer of 1999 was sunny and beautiful, but it passed very quickly. Some families began to think of returning to Kosova, and the first of them were able to do so in September. My own mother, who celebrated her eightieth birthday at that time, was able to return after four months. I was sad and depressed, and missed my relatives. But my pressure wound didn't heal as quickly as I hoped and I had to stay here. Fortunately, my depression didn't last long.

At that time, two families who had suffered terribly during the war arrived from Kosova. Seven family members had been killed and some of the surviving children were wounded. All of them received whatever help that they needed, including invaluable medical treatment.

In Meadow Court, life was following a normal pattern. Children began going to school and adults to college to learn English, and my own English began to improve. I found the opportunity to learn more about the culture, history, tradition and democratic system of this country very helpful.

In early November, all the people at Meadow Court were deeply saddened by the death of Adriana Hoxha Lamaxhema. She had struggled bravely with her illness for five months, and she will always be remembered not only by her family but by everybody who lived at Meadow Court.

On Remembrance Day, at a ceremony attended by the whole Meadow Court community, friends, working staff and local people, a tree, with an accompanying plaque, was planted in memory of those Kosovars who were killed in the war and to commemorate the refuge which others found in Altrincham.

Soon Christmas came and with it Father Christmas, bringing everyone lots of lovely presents and making the children in particular very happy.

After twenty-two months, the last family left Meadow Court. All of those who had not been able to return to Kosova settled in the local community. Meadow Court is now silent and empty but we will always remember it. It was a haven for us after a difficult period in our lives. But much more will we remember the people who helped us so much and the friends with whom we are still in contact. I hope that this record of our experience will help other people in need. The Kosovar refugees will certainly be grateful to the people of this country all their lives. Falemnderit . . .

Amir Lamaxhema

On 24 March 1999, when the NATO bombing campaign started, all Kosovar Albanians were finally convinced that western European countries had decided to take some action in order to prevent further atrocities in their country. On 14 January 1999, in Racak village, eleven kilometres away from my home town, Serbs had committed one of the worst massacres. Around fifty people were brutally killed when Serb police, military and paramilitary forces attacked the village.

Those who died were innocent farmers, most of them old people who were unable to escape. For all Albanians in Kosova, the general security situation got worse and worse. A lot of people were killed on the very first night of bombings. At that time I was working with the Organization for Security and Cooperation in Europe as an interpreter and security guards supervisor. Serbs had started hunting all local staff working with international observers. For that reason my family and I left our flat and sought shelter elsewhere. After eight days spent at my in-laws, we decided on 31 March to try to cross the border into Macedonia. Our first attempt was unsuccessful but on the following morning we managed to get on the train and, after four hours waiting at the border crossing, we were able to reach 'the promised land' called Macedonia.

After one and a half months my wife Adriana got sick and was admitted to a Tetova hospital. Having been examined there, she was diagnosed with leukaemia, though nobody told me so at the time. Five days later some English doctors, who came and visited Adriana, offered us the chance to go to the United Kingdom for further medical treatment. I was over the moon about that because the medical care in Macedonia was very bad.

On 19 May 1999 Adriana and I, my sister, father and mother, together with Adriana's family, left Macedonia and flew to the UK. After a three-hour flight we were notified that we were about to land in Manchester. I was excited for two reasons: first, because I knew that Adriana would get the treatment she needed and, second, because I was coming to the city of Manchester United FC, one of the best football clubs in the world. After all the other passengers had left the plane, doctors and nurses came on board and helped Adriana to the ambulance car which was waiting for us.

We drove to the refugee reception centre, where a large number of people – I later found out that they were social

workers – were waiting for us. We received a very hearty
welcome. It was as if they had known us for ages. Absolutely
everybody was at our service. Afterwards our pictures were
taken for refugee identifications and we had supper. It was
amazing how those wonderful people helped us that night; I
know that they were tired but nobody showed it at all. After
an hour spent there and after Adriana had had a medical
check-up, we were guided to a large room where we could
make phone calls. Later on social workers provided toiletries
for everybody and we were ready to leave the centre. After
a two-hour journey by bus we reached Ulverstone in the Lake
District. Throughout the trip Adriana had severe stomach
pain and she was very poorly, but a doctor stayed beside her
all the time. The others in our party were lodged temporarily
in an elementary school, but Adriana and myself were taken
to a hospital ten miles away. The doctors and nurses were
brilliant, and we spent two days there while our families were
still in Ulverstone. Then two women volunteers transported
our families from Ulverstone to Manchester and Adriana and
I were taken to Manchester Royal Infirmary, one of the best
hospitals in England. All the staff from Ward 27 were
wonderful to us, and even the other patients tried to help us
at every stage.

When our parents came to visit in the evening, I asked
them how they had got there. When they answered 'By taxi',
I was confused, for I knew that we had spent all our money
in Macedonia. But my father explained that Social Services
had taken care of the fare. It was another very nice surprise.
Everybody was trying to make us comfortable. Two days
later I went to see our new accommodation at Meadow Court,
Wellfield Lane in Hale. The building itself was owned by the
council, but the area was beautiful. The flats were small but
very suitable for us. We were the second group of refugees
to be situated in Meadow Court. The first families to be
lodged there were Ferizi, Alaj and Hashani.

Trafford Borough Council social workers were there with us all the time. They were the people I had met on the first day, and Barbara Donovan welcomed me and showed me the flat. It was a small flat but nice and cosy. All the necessary things, such as bedding, toiletries, etc. were provided that night. The following morning I met Bruce Thompson, the Methodist Church minister. Everybody from Meadow Court knew him and gathered to shake hands with him. I believe he was surprised and pleased that I could speak English. Since then, certainly, we have spent a lot of time together discussing all kinds of things. He used to come to Meadow Court almost every day and on each visit he brought things for the residents: toys for the children, clothes, bicycles, food and everything else we needed. People from his congregation also came to help us on a daily basis, with car boots full of useful items. Bruce and his people from the church became very, very close to us. His help was tremendous in every respect. He used to spend whole days with us and became one of us, a member, so to say, of every family in Meadow Court.

Bruce and I became very good friends, and I greatly valued his helpful advice. He organized trips for us to places like Old Trafford, Alton Towers and Chester Zoo, and arranged for us to swim at Altrincham Leisure Centre every Monday and to watch every home game at Altrincham FC. In addition, he used to come and pick up kids for football coaching and to invite us to his church for lunch and different games. He visited every family, brought bikes for their children and at Christmas saw that there were presents for everybody. In one word, he was a real hero. But he was not alone. People from the Altrincham Muslim Association also helped us very much. They used to organize picnics and came to visit us every day. And Adrian Flanagan, the owner of the local taxi company, continued to help us when his contract with Trafford Borough had expired.

In short, everybody tried to make us feel comfortable.

People from the neighbourhood were very kind to us, especially at the post office, farmhouse grocery and local butcher's. We actually never felt like refugees. We were treated like their own people, and that was something wonderful. They made us forget all the bad things we experienced in Kosova, and they were more than friends.

Bruce Thompson and people from Altrincham Muslim Association visited Adriana at the hospital many times. The night when Adriana passed away Amjad and Sayeed came to Manchester Royal Infirmary and drove us (myself and my in-laws) back to Meadow Court. Bruce was there, Barbara, Rita and Ann too. It was good to have them close when life was tough. Moreover, Bruce and the Altrincham Muslim Association helped me a lot about Adriana's funeral service and supported me with money and tickets when I was about to take her body to Kosova. For these people nothing seemed too much trouble, nothing was impossible. And it has meant a lot to me that the management of the Altrincham Football Club allowed me to train with their players and that the manager Bernard Taylor, coach Graham Heathcote and players such as Jason Gallagher and Danny Adams accepted me as one of their own. Finally, the financial support of the British Government when we were about to leave this wonderful country was much appreciated.

I am very grateful to everybody for everything they did for us and I would like to visit them again soon. May God bless all of them. It was an enormous privilege to have known them and their beautiful country.

Saranda Bogujevci

Something very unusual happened to me. I would not have believed it could happen, and not many children live through it. But it totally changed my situation and my life.

What happened was a war, but an unusual war, a war that

did not look like a war. I have read books about wars and seen films in which people have been killed in war-time. But I could not have imagined anything like that happening to me.

Even before the war, my life and that of my family was unlike that of people in the free world. Because foreigners ruled our country, I could not play in the street or go to school like other children. But I can remember lovely sunny days in my childhood when I played in the garden with my brothers, watched by my smiling parents. But then the war broke out and I had to stay inside the house, trying to distract my brothers from thinking about what could happen and watched by parents who now were anxious, tearful and helpless.

It is difficult to find words to describe how my parents must have felt. But I know that, above all, they wished that their children should survive. And, as I looked at my brothers, my parents and all the other relatives gathered in our house, it was my wish too. I said to myself: I don't care if I am killed, so long as my family can be safe. But that wasn't the way that things turned out. For I am alive but my brothers and my mother are not.

The day that the war ended was the happiest day and the saddest day of my life. But in order to explain what I mean when I say this, I must tell you more about myself.

I was born in Kosova and lived in a beautiful, big house in a large town called Podujeva. The school I went to was only fifteen minutes away, and as I walked there with my friends, having fun and laughing, the time passed very quickly. Later the journey seemed much longer – more like fifteen hours or days. You may wonder why. The answer is that we were afraid – afraid that the Serbs might come and take our school. And in the end that is what happened.

The Serbs thought that by taking our schools they would destroy our culture, our knowledge, our future. They thought that we would be left hanging about in the streets. But we were not to be defeated. We did not let ourselves down or our people or our country. We kept our education going by setting up a school in a damaged house. The students did not have chairs or desks and there was no electricity. But I was very happy there. Our teachers were very kind and we had lots of fun with them.

When I was six years old, my family moved to Sweden for a year and a half, and I have happy memories of mixing with other Kosovars working there, of attending a small international school, of beginning to learn Swedish and of enjoying the beautiful Swedish countryside. When we returned to Kosova, I entered year five at school and began to learn English, little thinking that I would come to England and speak English all the time. I also began to sing in a choir, for choral singing was important in the life of our community.

In 1998 the Serbs started the war because they wanted our land. They had already denied us our rights, thrown our people out of work and taken our schools. They wanted to destroy us, and our family suffered terribly. My mother, my two brothers, my grandmother, my cousin, my uncle's wife, my father's aunt and her daughter-in-law and my father's friend's family – all were killed. And on 28 March 1999 I was shot by Serbian soldiers. My four cousins, my uncle, my father and I are the only survivors.

At the time that I was shot, I did not want to live but I knew that I was not going to die. Two of my cousins were also shot, one in the arm and the other in the throat. We spent three months in hospital in Prishtina. The doctors and nurses in the hospital were Serbians and they did not look after us properly but treated us like animals.

After one month, my father found out where we were and came to visit us. To reach the hospital he had to walk for seven hours. He could not stay there because Serbian soldiers could have killed him, and he could not go home because of a similar threat from the soldiers and police who were there. So he walked back for seven hours to hide in the forest.

In the hospital I felt lonely and sometimes very scared. The building looked like a prison and felt like a prison. All the time I was hungry and thirsty and did not feel like a patient in a hospital.

After three months, KFOR (Kosovo Force – the UN force) came to Kosova, the Serbian soldiers and police had to return to Yugoslavia and I was able to leave hospital. In Prishtina hospital, my cousins and I met an English doctor who arranged for us to come to England for medical treatment. I came to England with my uncle, my cousins and my father, and one injured cousin and I went straight to hospital, while the others were taken to Meadow Court, where the other Kosovar refugees were housed.

The end of the war was something to which I reacted in two different ways. I was glad that my injuries could be properly treated, but I was also very, very sad to have lost so many members of my family and to have had to leave others in Kosova. The situation would have been very different if, before the war, I had been coming with my family for a holiday in England. I would have been very excited. But, after all that had happened in the war, adjustment to a new country was difficult for me.

My cousin and I have been in and out of hospital in Manchester for necessary operations, and the doctors and nurses have been caring and skilful. In our room in the hospital, we had TV, videos and tapes, whereas in Prishtina we didn't even have enough food to eat. My father has remarried and, now that I am out of hospital, I live in a flat with my dad, my stepmother (herself a Kosovar) and my new baby brother. But my cousin and I still have to go to hospital every week for physiotherapy.

After four months in England, I started school here, and I have found the teachers very generous and the students very friendly. Indeed, I think that coming to England has been very good for me – after all, if I hadn't come, I would probably have lost my arm. And I like the place, the people, the school – everything, in fact, except the weather! My family are beginning to feel settled, and I am myself stronger and have new hopes for my life.

After we had been in England for a year and a half, my dad decided to take us back to Kosova for three weeks. A special ceremony had been arranged in the local town hall to remember the members of our family who had been killed, and he wanted to be there. We flew from Heathrow and, after a good trip, we were greeted by an excited crowd of friends and relatives. When we reached my home town, I went straight to my grandmother's, and she was delighted to see that my arm is better, that I am stronger and that, at sixteen, I am more grown up! I stayed at my home with my dad, and my aunt came to keep us company. The house was so quiet, so empty without my mum, my brothers and my other relatives.

The memorial ceremony was held on 28 March. It was very painful to look at the pictures of my brothers, my cousins and four other children, with the candles in front of them. I felt that I was having a bad dream, and I wasn't sure when it would end. For the rest of my stay in Kosova, I tried not to think of what had happened in the past and to enjoy the company of my family and friends.

On my return to England, I was greeted by smiling faces. But the folk I had left behind were in tears. For in my country, the people are without homes, without schools and, in some cases, without food. I hope that their needs will soon be met, and that the war in Kosova will be the last war ever. I hope too that my arm will soon be completely healed and that I will be able to go back to Kosova and start a new life.

Meanwhile, I am grateful for the kindness of all the people I met at Meadow Court and especially Bruce, the Methodist minister. I particularly enjoyed the parties and trips, some of which – for example, the expedition to the Trafford Centre which is described in this book – were very exciting. But I also learned a great deal because, though I am not a Christian, I began to attend the Methodist church and still go to services there. I learned that if you love, you live. It does not matter what faith you profess, there is only one God. He knows why he created us and why there are different religions, cultures and languages. And the variety is stimulating. That is why, though I am a Muslim, I go to church. My life is enriched by learning about another approach to religion and to life. And I am better prepared for whatever surprises tomorrow may bring. For, as I have learned from hard experience, life is very short and you don't know when, where or how you will die.

Epilogue

13

A Promise Fulfilled

For two simple reasons, I felt a great need to visit Kosova. In the first place, I had heard and read so much about the country that I yearned to see it at first hand; and secondly, and more importantly, I had a promise to keep.

It was to Naim and Shpresa that I made that promise, on the night when Nevrije waited on us with melons and chi and Shpresa asked, 'Why do you do this for my people?' 'One day,' I said, 'we'll have a drink together in Kosova.' The war was still at its height and it was extraordinary, if not foolish, to suggest that one day we would be together in a country that was being ethnically cleansed by Serb forces and pounded day and night by NATO war-planes.

But in the summer of 2001, two years after the doors of Meadow Court first opened, I was preparing to fulfil that promise. Time and again the Kosovars had urged me to go back 'home' with them, to receive their hospitality and to see their homeland. And the dream that it might become possible was about to be realized.

Thanks to the generosity of the Methodist Church, I received financial help and the opportunity to take a sabbatical, and I flew out to Kosova with Selatin and his two sons Fatos and Genc. In the preceding weeks I had fought off many invitations to stay in many homes. Selatin, in particular, pressed me and even bought tickets for the same flights as myself. But as soon as Naim and Shpresa heard that I was to go to Kosova, they hastily arranged to be there before me, even though, to do so, they had to spent three days in Frankfurt en route!

It was an emotional moment when, at Prishtina airport, I stepped down on to Kosovan soil. I made a double check that I had arrived, glancing down at my feet and up at the surrounding hills. Once through passport control, I was over-joyed to see Naim in the waiting crowd, his eyes glistening. Selatin and his boys were greeted as warmly by his own family and, with what appeared to be some reluctance, he finally accepted that I would be staying with Naim and his family.

We were driven to Mitrovica by Naim's brother-in-law Vedat. Two years earlier, we had tried, but failed, to bring him, his wife Besa, and his two boys Exon and Erdit to England, and later that night we were all to sit around a crowded table and to reflect, in our own ways, on the efforts that had been made. It was, for me, a healing moment. The family's predicament and my failure to help them had tortured me during the war. But now they were welcoming me to the home of Vedat's brother.

His was the only house belonging to the family that remained standing after the Serb destruction of Albanian Mitrovica. Vedat's mother had stayed behind in Mitrovica while her three sons and their respective families had fled the Serb onslaught. The fact that, though married to an Albanian, she was herself a Serb enabled her to send the young paramili-taries away with a flea in their ear each time they called. Little did they know that, in her back courtyard, she was sheltering two frightened Albanian teenage boys who had been separ-ated from their families. She had not known them before the war but what she did was typical of what happened elsewhere in the country, as folk shared what little they had and offered shelter and food to strangers. Hers was the first of many enlightening and deeply moving stories that made my trip to Kosova so worthwhile and memorable.

My time in Kosova was neatly split into two: I spent the first half in the north in Mitrovica and the second half in the south in Gjilan. I began by visiting places that I had seen on the television news or read about in the newspapers and by meeting fascinating people with amazing stories to tell; and then, in the south, I met a number of folk who had travelled back to Kosova and, at the same time, saw many refugees fleeing their homes under a barrage of Macedonian artillery fire.

Mitrovica was an extraordinary place. It resembled a post-apocalyptic world, one of which those who design sets for fantasy movies would have been justly proud. But this was not fantasy, this was for real. Little strings of lights hung over shop windows to help the passer-by, and crowds of people, many of whom were trying to escape from the even harsher conditions in the countryside, roamed the streets. Rubble from destroyed homes lined the dirt tracks that acted as roads. The infrastructure appeared to have been completely ruined. But time and again I was told how much had been accomplished since the war. Seeing the conditions two years later, one shuddered to think what the situation had been like at its worst.

Mitrovica is divided by a river, the Serbs now living in the northern half of the city and the Albanians in the south. The bridges which link the two communities are guarded by French soldiers and constitute a modern Check Point Charlie. The fact that this must be one of the most volatile places in the region was underlined by what happened when I tried to take a photograph. A soldier pulled his gun on me, and the sound of the safety catch coming off remains clear in my mind. As I have mentioned before, I failed French O Level twice, but at last my French teacher would have been proud of me as I defused the situation. In the end, the soldier even wanted to have his picture taken with me!

A visit to Skënderaj brought back memories of a repeated TV documentary which I had seen in February 1999. The programme, entitled *Death in the Valley*, dealt with the siege that led to fifty members of the Jashari family being killed by

Serb forces. And here I was visiting what remained of the village and drinking chi with a surviving member of the family. It was humbling to answer questions about how the Scottish and Welsh Assemblies could come into being without bloodshed and to hear a very genuine concern for Northern Ireland expressed. A strange day, to say the least.

While in Mitrovica I met two Roman Catholics, a priest and a religious sister. The scene resembled an episode in Simon Winchester's *The Fracture Zone*, a book well worth reading by those wanting both to be strangely entertained and, at the same time, to learn about the bloody history of the Balkans. It was a humid afternoon shortly after a downpour. The sister was peeling vegetables in the courtyard behind the church and in front of the presbytery. Two women seemed to be watching and waiting for something to happen, and a dog was taking an unhealthy interest in a bitch that had just given birth to five pups. Children, who were playing a game nearby, stopped to stare at their visitor. One of the women was despatched to make chi, while the other was sent to fetch the priest. Half an hour later the priest appeared. We had clearly disturbed his siesta, for he was still in what appeared to be night clothes and he had yet to find his teeth. But appearances belied great faith and courage. The priest and the sister, who had sent Serb paramilitaries packing on more than one occasion, were held in high regard by the local Albanians. The priest had repeatedly declared that God had sent him to this parish and, if he were to die there, then so be it. And he probably would have died if the paramilitaries had known that he and the sister were sheltering two Albanian families in the presbytery. As it was, before the paramilitaries departed they beat the sister, leaving a large deep scar which she covered with a headscarf.

One man, a shopkeeper, wanted me to know his story. When trudging the road to the border, carrying his five-year-old daughter in his arms, he saw paramilitaries ahead and the body of an Albanian lying beside them. He shielded his daughter from the scene but later she asked why it was that the man was lying in the road. He replied that he was drunk. 'But he had been bleeding,' she said. 'He bumped his nose,' he answered. 'No, Daddy, he was dead. Why lie to me?' Later, near the border, the family was given bread by a Serb soldier. When, on hearing of atrocities, the father expressed hatred for all Serbs, the little girl recalled the soldier and the help given, saying, 'How can we hate someone who helped us, Daddy?' The man wanted me to know how wonderful children are at expressing the truth.

The shopkeeper's brother spent an afternoon with me detailing his time in a Serb prison. He had only been released two months before, having been incarcerated, without trial or reason, for almost two years. He told me of the massacre of 148 of his fellow inmates. Some had tried to climb vertical walls to escape the bullets, while others had clawed at a manhole cover. But when the cover was lifted, their efforts were to no avail. A grenade was dropped down upon them. I shall never forget these stories.

But the most harrowing experience was provided by my visit to Podujeva, the home village of the Bogujevci family. Selatin was waiting for Naim, Vedat and myself as we drove down the muddy main street. The pot holes, other cars and pedestrians threatened to make us stop, but we got through. After a wonderful meal we stood on the doorstep and looked at a tower in the distance from which a sniper had sought to pick off the Bogujevci family. Eventually they had been rounded up, frog marched to the police station, detained there for a while, marched back down the street, pushed through a gate in a wall and lined up to be shot. To take that walk and to stand in what was an otherwise beautiful and tranquil garden was painful in the extreme. The family had stood in front of a large red rose bush, and its petals, now lying across the ground, seemed to symbolize the blood which had been shed. Could there be a more poignant reminder of what had happened there two years previously? Eighteen people had been shot and only a handful, including the Bogujevci children whom I knew so well, had survived.

Enver, Selatin's neighbour, journeyed with us to the cemetery and to an unmarked plot of land within it. There he told me of the day he had left the other men in the mountains, twenty to thirty thousand of them in hiding from the paramilitaries. He had heard of a massacre in Podujeva and had gone back to the village. Finding it deserted, he had wandered around until he stumbled upon the paramilitaries in the cemetery. He went straight up to them and surprised them by his presence. The leader asked what he was doing there. Enver told him he was looking for his family but couldn't find them. On being asked their names, he dutifully furnished the man with the information. 'For two thousand marks I will show you where they are,' the paramilitary offered. Enver only had one thousand but the man agreed that it was enough. On receiving the money, the man stood to one side and pointed to the bulldozer just completing the task of covering up the bodies. Enver had lost his parents, his wife and three children. It was vitally important to him that others should know of his plight. I assured him that I would not forget him, and we parted with huge hugs, tears and genuine smiles.

The second half of my visit to Kosova was spent in the south and I concentrated, for the most part, on trying to link up with some of those who had returned home shortly after the war. The first such reunion came in a village known as Gadime. Selami, Shpresa's brother, had phoned on ahead to inform the Hashani family that we would be arriving some time on the Saturday. When we reached the village, Selami asked the first man we saw where the Hashani family lived: 'They're all Hashani's here! Which Hashani?' On hearing that we had come with news of Remzi in England, the man instantly hailed a small boy on a bicycle to act as our guide.

He led us along a dusty track to a large house, from which a crowd of people spilled out and rushed towards us. Before I could get out of the car, Mrs Hashani was walking towards me, as the family created a kind of tunnel for her to pass through. Here was the old lady whom we had lost, in full Albanian dress, on that wonderful day in Chester two years before. And then, just as we had all sat down in the house, first Banush and then Remzi phoned from Manchester. To picture them in Manchester while sitting in their Kosovar home with the mother whom they adore and whom they remain desperate to see was a memorable moment indeed.

Two days later we were with the Lamaxhema family in Ferizaj. We had arranged to meet Nesim and Amir outside the Crystal Hotel in Gjilan, and our reunion was exciting and satisfying beyond words. We then travelled together to their home just a few miles away, passing American troops tidying up the pavement in a little village with a busy market. The troops, like all their colleagues in Kosova, were in full combat gear with the temperature around 28 degrees centigrade. I had almost grown used to the fact that troops patrolled the streets as if in a combat zone. But armoured vehicles in convoys heading towards the Macedonian border and cars loaded with people and possessions heading in the opposite direction into Kosova heightened the tension in the air. Hostilities between Macedonian Albanians and government forces had increased, and I had already met a family who had fled the artillery bombardment, leaving the father behind. But now things appeared to be worsening. Though such circumstances were not exactly unfamiliar, the significant difference was that, on this occasion, I was much closer to the situation.

Walking through Ferizaj was a truly humbling experience. Nesim and Amir introduced me to pedestrians and shopkeepers as 'The minister from Manchester'. Since some of them had seen a video of the TV documentary that had focused on the work of Meadow Court, I was recognized, hugged and kissed by complete strangers. I was even given ice creams for myself and everyone with me – not just any old ice creams but the best in the freezer!

We stood at Adriana's grave. It was a time of reflection for me on yet another momentous day. All the conversations in the hospital and the telephone calls from holiday, as I tried to encourage Adriana in her plight, came flooding back. Around her lay the graves of young men and women, boys and girls who had died during and shortly after the war. I did not know any of them, but their ages alone were tragically eloquent. And I did know something of Adriana's story. She had always wanted to return home, and now she was home, and at peace.

On the way back from the cemetery I spotted the local Catholic church. A sister was tending the garden. I felt compelled to enter. My companions – Amir, and Selatin and his nephew, who had joined us for the day – followed. When we reached the top of the steps, we began to remove our shoes, and the sister rushed over. There was no need, she said, to remove our shoes. This was a church, not a mosque! We told her how dirty our shoes were and removed them all the same. She appeared to understand and left us to our visit. We sat on the front row. There was a pregnant pause, and the silence was breathtaking and deeply refreshing. I felt that I should say something. But what? The advice of a wise sister to a young novice came to mind. When asked when it is appropriate to break the silence, the sister replied, 'Only when you can improve upon it'. Any words that I could offer would certainly not improve the silence. But the words of another might. When I walked over to the lectern, my companions again followed. We stood in a circle as I scanned the shelf below the desk. At last I found what I was looking for. I passed the Albanian Bible to Amir and asked him to read these words.

My soul glorifies the Lord
and my spirit rejoices in God my Saviour,
for he has been mindful of the humble state of his servant.
From now on all generations will call me blessed,
for the Mighty One has done great things for me – holy
  is his name.
His mercy extends to those who fear him,
from generation to generation.
He has performed mighty deeds with his arm;
he has scattered those who are proud in their inmost
  thoughts.
He has brought down rulers from their thrones
  but has lifted up the humble.
He has filled the hungry with good things
but has sent the rich away empty.
He has helped his servant Israel,
  remembering to be merciful
to Abraham and his descendants for ever,
even as he said to our fathers. (Luke 1.46–55)

Having explained that these words were recorded by the early
Church to express Mary's joy at the news that she was to
give birth to Jesus, I asked Amir to read the words that Jesus
quoted from Isaiah in his sermon at Nazareth:

The Spirit of the Lord is on me,
  because he has anointed me
    to preach good news to the poor.
He has sent me to proclaim freedom for the prisoners
    and recovery of sight for the blind,
to release the oppressed,
to proclaim the year of the Lord's favour. (Luke 4.18–19)

Selatin's nephew was quiet and reflective for the rest of
the day. Later, as I was about to leave, he asked Amir to

tell me that never before had he heard such beautiful words.

Though my stay in Kosova had been brief, I longed to see my wife and our two boys again. But even with the help of that experience and of all the other things I have heard and seen, I still struggle to conceive how the Kosovars felt when forced from their homeland, not knowing when, if ever, they would return.

There were many things, however, that became clearer to me during my time in Kosova, and the events of 11 September 2001 gave them greater significance.

First, the importance of history. It seems to me that we have undervalued history in recent years. During the Cold War all was quite clear. The enemy was over there, we were over here; they were the baddies, we were the goodies. When communism collapsed we thought we were about to enter a new age, and we failed to recognize that many would revisit their past. When, therefore, old enmities resurfaced and new hostilities broke out, we discovered that, like the people scolded by Jeremiah, we had cried 'Peace, peace' when there was no peace.

Today we lay great stress on economics and science. We are often led by economists and scientists, not by statesmen and historians. Mathematics appears to have a far greater importance than history in the National Curriculum. Yet how are we to understand the present if we don't fully appreciate our past? If the future is to be less threatening, we must dig deep into the past and reflect fully upon it.

Second, the paramount need to distribute the earth's resources fairly. It cannot be right that one-fifth of the world's population should enjoy four-fifths of the world's wealth. Nor can it be right that, while so many go hungry, people are employed to remove and discard food from our supermarket shelves which is past its sell-by date. Is it any wonder that the poor and oppressed become envious of our life-style? I recall reading an interview with the news presenter George

Alagiah, who possesses a picture of shanty huts in Rio as a reminder of his time there. Each of the roofs appears to have a television aerial. His point was that we cannot go on beaming images of our decadent life-style around the globe without the poor wanting a slice of the cake. Jesus tells his disciples to invite to a party those who cannot invite them back rather than those who can repay them in kind. To many in the world we in the West appear to be enjoying one huge party. The question is whether we have the faith and courage to invite them to join us.

Third, the sinister significance of the increase of bigotry. I returned to a country that had just experienced a general election, in which race appeared to have played an important part. Race riots had erupted in many northern cities, and the number of votes cast for the British National Party had increased substantially. Bigotry is alive in the Balkans, and I have seen its consequences. Because it is also present and on the increase in these islands, it needs to be challenged, whenever and wherever it appears, especially in the Christian Church. I have heard outrageously sweeping statements about 'Muslims and Jews' in services and church meetings. I have heard entire races described as 'people of darkness while we are people of light'. We have much to learn and much to do. The cost is great but the reward greater still.

The life and teaching of Martin Luther King remains influential for many. I recall how one night he returned late from a meeting. He was tired out and went to bed. The phone rang and he heard what he described as an 'ugly voice', saying, 'Nigger, if you're not out of town in x days I'm going to blow your brains out.' Martin Luther King had heard this sort of threat many times before but that night it 'got' to him. He looked at his wife asleep beside him and his beautiful newborn daughter in the cot at the foot of the bed and realized how quickly he could be taken from them or they from him. He could not sleep and went to the kitchen to pour himself a coffee. As he hung his head over the cup, he felt a presence in the room with him. A voice said, 'Martin stand up for righteousness, stand up for justice, stand up for truth.' From that moment Martin Luther King was ready to face whatever lay ahead.

Few of us have such a powerful experience of God's presence and such a clear directive. But we know in our heart of hearts that we are to love our neighbours, whoever they are and in whatever circumstances they find themselves.

In Kosova I found myself turning time and again to my Bible and to the account of Simon of Cyrene being press-ganged into carrying the cross of a complete stranger. Simon had no choice. He had to carry Jesus' cross. Often in the previous two years I had considered that my role at Meadow Court was freely to take up my own cross and follow the teaching of Jesus. I came to see, however, that I and others had been enabled to respond to the needs of others by the redemptive love of Christ, of which his cross is the sign and symbol.

14

Guidelines

These guidelines may be helpful to churches considering commitment to a project like that described in this book.

It is important that CHURCHES should:

- make the whole venture a matter of prayer;

- dare to dream and have the courage to turn that dream into reality;

- acknowledge that, no matter how large or small the church and how many or how few church members are involved, success will depend upon partnership with other organizations;

- make contact and establish links with those organizations, e.g. associations, churches, charities, other faith communities and the local authority, as early as possible;

- recognize that everyone in the church has a potential contribution to make and that many people who cannot be involved for the duration of the project will be able to undertake specific tasks when needed;

- reflect constantly, using the full range of relevant resources: scripture, faith, and such knowledge as they have or can acquire about the history and culture of those in need and the immediate causes of their problems;

- aim, when addressing the needs of people of another faith, to support the community which is closest to them in religion rather than to take the lead themselves;

- forget 'in-your-face evangelism', since what Christians are, rather than what they say, is crucial, especially where the victims of desperate situations are concerned;

- be prepared gladly to receive as well as to give;

- strive to empower rather than to manage both the helpers and those they seek to help;

- acknowledge that, as time goes by, needs will change and that there is a right time for everything;

- resist the temptation to overwhelm those in need with unfocused and unrealistic generosity, remembering how in Timperley the database prevented the collection of unnecessary items;

- refuse to be guilt-ridden about failures along the way, never forgetting that the important thing is to have tried.

It is equally important that CO-ORDINATORS should:

- be open and honest;

- be accountable to a wise, independent counsellor;

- love their neighbours – and themselves, setting aside time for relaxation, reflection and renewal;

- be humble enough to accept wise suggestions and strong enough to resist negative attitudes;

- accept, with gratitude, that this may be the most significant task – for themselves and for others – that they will ever undertake.

Notes

1. Thomas G. Pettepiece, 'Visions of a World Hungry' in *A Guide to Prayer for Ministers and other Servants* (Upper Room 1983).
2. Later I was to read Desmond Tutu's *No Future without Forgiveness* (Random House 1999). In this account of South Africa's Truth and Reconciliation Commission, Tutu acknowledges the extra burdens carried by the interpreters, who had to convey the testimony of both victims and perpetrators.
3. The distance between Tirana and Meadow Court was abruptly shortened one evening when, to my amazement, I saw a TV news report, complete with pictures of the studio and the presenters, about the service which was being provided.
4. Quoted in *The Holocaust: Faith, Morality and Ethics* (Holocaust Educational Trust).
5. The phrase 'Chetnik forces' was a bone of contention for many people but, after much debate, it was finally accepted.
6. Michael Ignatieff, *Virtual War: Kosovo and Beyond* (Chatto & Windus 2000).
7. Misty Bernall, *She Said Yes: The Unlikely Martyrdom of Cassie Bernall* (Plough 1999).
8. Quoted in Tony Kushner and Katherine Knox, *Refugees in an Age of Genocide* (Frank Cass 1999).